SEASONS OF BLOOD

by

HENRY BEISSEL

BuschekBooks
Ottawa

Copyright © 2011 Henry Beissel
All rights reserved.

Library and Archives Canada Cataloguing in Publication

Beissel, Henry, 1929-
Seasons of blood / Henry Beissel.

Poems.
ISBN 978-1-894543-67-5

I. Title.

PS8503.E39S43 2011 C811'.54 C2011-902333-4

Cover art: *Traumatic II*, mixed media painting by Arlette Francière.

Printed in Winnipeg, Manitoba by Hignell Book Printing.

MIX
Paper from responsible sources
FSC
www.fsc.org FSC® C013916

BuschekBooks, P.O. Box 74053, 5 Beechwood Avenue
Ottawa, Ontario, Canada K1M 2H9
www.buschekbooks.com

BuschekBooks gratefully acknowledges the support of the Canada Council for the Arts for its publishing program.

Canada Council for the Arts   Conseil des Arts du Canada

Table of Contents

    Spring: Bloodroot

1. The Ides of March   9
2. April Fools   21
3. May Song and Dance   35

    Summer: The Devil's Club

4. Where Shall the Birds Fly?   51
5. When Africa Calls Uhuru   82
6. Across the Sun's Warp   127

Introduction

I think there is a similarity here between Henry Beissel and Joseph Conrad, another foreign writer who became a country gentleman and adopted English as his writing language of choice. Both survived childhoods of disaster: Conrad, the Russian pogroms against Polish nationalists and intellectuals, which took the life of his father; Beissel, the war years of Hitler's Germany, with its false dreams, deprivations and eventual fire-bombings, followed by a legacy of shame. Both writers developed what has been described as a spectacular view of the universe. For Conrad, the universe was spectacle both cruel and benign, where mankind would ultimately freeze in the dark, but nonetheless worthy awe and wonder and intense study. For Henry Beissel, living in the countryside in Eastern Ontario, the natural world, with its abundant creatures and changing seasons, was a constant presence, more sustaining than debilitating, more entertainment than irritant. In this milieu, with the nourishing influence of family and admiring students, he casts a discerning eye on the political world unfolding around him. Like Conrad, he is appalled by ignorance and folly, but mostly by man's inhumanity to man, his indignation further fuelled by a need for the world to eradicate all signs reminding him of the crimes and depredations of his birthplace.

Beissel's early years in Canada included study at the University of Toronto, work for CBC radio, travels in the arctic and, eventually, a career as a university teacher, writer and editor. *Edge*, the title of a publication he founded and edited from the University of Alberta in Edmonton, is, perhaps, an indicator of his perceptions of his place in the universe at that time: edgy, haunting the margins, but hopefully part of a literary and cultural avant-garde, being on the 'cutting edge.' And, indeed, the writings that flowed from the technologies he inherited—pen, typewriter and computer—show a man determined to give imaginative shape not only to his own demons, but to ours as well. I had the pleasure of publishing *Under Coyote's Eye*, his brilliant play about Ishi, the last surviving member of the Yahi tribe in California, and his translations of the work of German poet Peter Huchel, an outsider silenced by the East German government. Not one to limit himself to success as a playwright and translator, Beissel embarked on an ambitious career as an epic poet, producing a remarkable sequence called *Cantos North*, in which he celebrates both the starkness, cold, novelty and relative purity of Canada's northlands, where perhaps a new breed of humans might be formed.

Seasons of Blood is no less epic in its ambitions, taking on, like Conrad, the world of greed and material interests. It's a bold, impassioned plea to forsake the conflicts and wars that are the legacy of this blindness, in exchange for an immersion in nature and love. Yet the nature Beissel presents here is not just nurturing and beautiful, it's violent and cataclysmic, where winter is "not a season / but a destiny for every sun" and where spring, we are told, "leaves a train / of blood / up and down / paths of renewal." Not an easy path, since the mind must journey "on pain of death / to reach fulfilment." In the face of these challenges, the poet asks:

> *Is there not ecstasy enough*
> *in this perpetual holocaust of creation*
> *for a love to encompass all?*

Apparently not, as the rhetorical question is quickly overwhelmed by memories of rape, starvation, torture and murder, the ground of which lies somewhere between T.S. Eliot's *Wasteland*, where "April is the cruellest month, breeding lilacs / out of the dead land," and Chaucer's more benign vision in *The Canterbury Tales*, where the soft showers of April "bathed every vein in swich / licour."

Seasons of Blood is, in many ways, a literary tour de force, moving from a richly textured and colloquial free verse to lines that are subtly rhymed and metrical. The range of reference is phenomenal, from Shakespeare to particle physics. E.J. Pratt and Christopher Dewdney aside, no other poet in Canada has such a profound interest in science and its vocabularies. Historically, *Seasons of Blood* has no shortage of tragic material to explore, including the Holocaust, the Falklands War, death squads in Guatemala and El Salvador, the bombing of Hiroshima, and the Israeli/Palestinian conflict which resulted in the September 1982 massacres at Sabra and Shatila refugee camps in Lebanon. These conflicts are mostly attributed to vested interests dividing the world into "hemispheres of power."

Though steeped in literary and biblical images, Henry Beissel's epic provides no religious consolation; instead, it is a wake-up call to "fools of faith," who have forgotten the essence of their belief systems and taken up arms and economics to enforce their versions of the truth. He reminds us, alluding to Matthew 6: 24-29, to consider instead the birds of the air and lilies of the field. In a world that is fast destroying its creatures and eco-systems, his work reminds me of those musicians on the stern of a sinking *Titanic* who, faced with an ultimate choice, rejected both terror and silence and instead struck up their instruments to belt out the message of amazing grace. And it's grace that abounds in this book, the grace of loving attention riveted to a dying world and the grace of language so finely tuned it breaks the heart while it nests in the ear.

Gary Geddes

The blood-dimmed tide is loosed, and everywhere
The ceremony of innocence is drowned;
The best lack all conviction, while the worst
Are full of passionate intensity.

     W. B. Yeats, "The Second Coming"

*These poems are dedicated to the victims
of our greed and folly everywhere.*

Spring: Bloodroot

1. *The Ides of March*

Beware. Mornings are brutal now
as they shatter the illusions of night
with a fierceness that stabs the eye.
  The sky leaps into the brain.

        We cannot escape spring.

An arrow of wild geese shrieks northward
in slow motion, piercing our dreams
quick with the point of their cries.

        We hear the warning.
        We smell the body odours
        of our beloved, earth.
        We know the morning
        of another season
        has come and that
        we cannot escape spring.

Spruce and fir throw quills of light,
the crusted snow cracks, and with its hard
bristles the westwind begins to sweep up
winter's shards. Slowly this well-tempered
planet tilts against the sun.

        A hundred millions years ago
        the cortex began to stir
        in obscure convolutions between
        hearing and smelling, a flesh
        cauliflower sprouting towards
        pressing the skull swelling
        reaching for...
            the light
        is coming we cannot escape
        though more than half of us
        is still in the dark. —A scream!...
        Listen!...
        Was that the last cry
        of six-year old Rosita
        beheaded with a machete
        after they hacked off her feet

in the Redeemer's land?
Or was it her mother
as they flayed her thighs?
Or her father as they
punctured his eyes? El Salvador
screamed and no one listened
at the equinox of blood
when military forces violated
all the laws of life and liberty
it took a billion springs to grow.
The power the blind have over the blind
is fearful. Money cannot endure
innocence. Cry, my beloved!
Rosita's eyes are rigid now.

Here the scream was a skyblue flutter
in bleak branches, a puff of snow—
a pair of jays warning the stillness
against predators. Birds
are forever startled
into flight sudden as
death because they know
freedom is in the air.
Or have they been frightened
by the coming of creatures
who hunt the hunted for a fee
for a trophy for a laugh kill
partridges polar-bears people?—
I have a message for you: the killers
are here. What happens in El Salvador
happens here in our hearts.

Gunships erupt over Guazapa.
The ancient volcano is still
but not the violence in the eyes
of men screaming bloody
murder blindness blossoming
into bullets rockets bombs
bursting into executions:
fire fuego FIRE!
consuming those who seek
freedom on this scorched earth.

Vietnam. Afghanistan. Poland. El Salvador. The redhot lava
of violence has seared every side of the mountain of history
and still it flows into the streets of villages, towns and
cities, threatening to suffocate and burn us all. The ashes
of unbridled power that bury us preserve our minds forever
twisted like those contorted bodies of Pompeii still clutching
their gold with their last charred cry. Cry, my beloved,

                                        cry to the stars!
                                 The morning is turning
                                 its back on Andromeda
                                 our next-door galaxy
                                 a couple of million light years
                                 down the road to eternity
                                 where winter is not a season
                                 but a destiny for every sun.

But here dawn and dew begin
their rousing glassbead game.
A flock of redpolls is pecking
a patch of hard ground
as if impatient to wake up
the earth where deep in darkness
the roots of maples sense
the sweetness of another season.

                                 The snow is melting.
                                 The sap is running.
                                 We cannot escape spring.
                                 The light will soon
                                 match the darkness
                                 and we must take sides.

Slowly the sun is hurtling
through the constellation of the fishes
that will not feed the multitude.
Soon it will reach its vernal equinox
to plant a garden in the north
that is the toil of many
but the delight of few.
The poor are poor
because the rich are rich
in a world divided
into hemispheres of power.

                              This is the month Champlain
                              sailed for a new and better
                              world and found Cain's land.
                              Others sailed before and after
                              on the tides of gold and glory,
                              somnambulists of freedom
                              bent on divine rule, driven by
                              the prevailing winds of politics
                              their hopes inflamed by a fever
                              of conquest and curiosity among
                              drifting continental plates
                              to spread a deadly virus
                              that hollows the heart and
                              strikes the mind with blindness.
                              Columbus was a carrier. So was
                              the Mayflower with its cargo
                              of heavenly pride. Half a millennium
                              of blood and bondage as the blind
                              led the blind up and down the Americas
                              into darkness. Civilization put to
                              the sword as far south as *Tierra del Fuego*.

And still men and women
drag the chains of their poverty
up and down the continent.
And still El Salvador is un-
redeemed—even in the sleep
of children who starve to death
in a nightmare of paradise
which Fourteen Families have turned
into hell. Land of plenty plundered
by the few. There is always a lord
to make a slave of his brother
by the blood ties of fear. Fifty
years of military dictatorships
and still their dreams live on.

                              Fifty civilians now murdered
                              every day and night between
                              hibiscus and banana flowers
                              by the national security forces
                              combing groves of cane citrus
                              and coffee up and down volcanic

slopes in pursuit of torture and
murder across rivers of steaming
sweat the innocent hiding in valleys
hunted between balsam cacao millet
beans and grapefruit by helicopters
spitting fire death—and everywhere
Rosita's rigid eyes watching
the seeds of freedom grow.

Mornings scream into consciousness
on the blue wings of jays.
Patches of snow are still holding out
deep in the north shadow
of spruce and cedar where
the sun cannot reach yet.

Heat and light are points
of violence in the brutal
wasteland of interstellar
space, a caprice of the cosmos
beyond our ken, a quick gesture
into the void. The sun is a nuclear
explosion among a hundred billion
others burning into extinction
at the speed of light.
Remember the moon.

The dying of a star quickens our hearts.
This galaxy has granted us a niche
on the edge of one of its spiral arms,
a space of time measured in generations
only, an equilibrium of day and night,
a balance of elements compounded
to flower into love and comprehension. It's that
or ashes. Mind or mineral—that is the question
in Rosita's eyes, and you and I must answer
to the difference between spring and winter.

Beware when eagles spread
their wings. This is the two-faced
month of Mars, god of warriors
and ploughmen. Blood is his
colour. A virgin was his

                    bride. And they danced
                    beating time
                    on the ground
                    with sword and share
                    as the sun entered its season.
                    We cannot escape spring.

Already the crocus bulbs
can feel the distant
light and shoots begin
to push the darkness
the whole length
of an owl's cry.
Sap runs to the ends
of poplar branches and
pussywillows punctuate
the budding bush
that gives refuge
to all the hunted
creatures of the world.

                    Here where honking geese put down for the night
                    on their annual pilgrimage to the pole, partridges
                    strut with dogged stealth the ancient mating paths;
                    deer shelter their vulnerable births against wolves.

Beware the Ides of March.
In the twilight eyes are
trained in the sights of blood.

                    Shoot her once
                    and shoot her twice
                    and shoot her once again
                    it's been a long long way
                    to El Progreso where Rosita saw
                    her twisted body slashed nipples cut
                    off limbs broken eyes dislodged jelly
                    saw on her way to school the muti-
                    lated strange woman toenails
                    painted dark poinsettias
                    in a torn tattered pink dress
                    in a roadside ditch the first of many
                    victims in the province of Usulután

                    in a crusted pool of blood
                    sacrifices to El Salvador in
                    a state of advanced putrefaction,
                    a black flock of zopilotes
                    feasting on her entrails. Ask
                    the vultures if they pecked out
                    the tongue that sang a hungry child
                    to sleep before it learnt to curse
                    the praetorians, scourge of all people.
                    And the question sprang from the black holes
                    in the gaping head and took root in
                    Rosita's eyes which had never known
                    winter till it became fixed there
                    forever demanding an answer.

The beaver wakes in his timbered winter fortress
as the creek cracks into shards of ice with the
fury of gunshots and shakes a flock of crows
like black fruit from the branches of an ash. Dark caw
wheels of fate spinning in the winds of a new season
turning men of reason into respectable monsters.

                         Blind man, where are you taking us?
                         Can't you hear the children crying
                         the tortured screaming
                         the moans of men and women
                         maimed because you will not
                         make them free
                         dying because you will not
                         feed them?
                         Can't you smell the stench of
                         decomposing flesh
                         drifting among orange blossoms?
                         The brain has a hundred trillion
                         circuits—is there not a single one
                         to connect someone else's pain
                         to your own compassion?
                         Are you nothing but a dream
                         in two dimensions?
                         Let Hollywood be forever
                         in and about Hollywood.
                         Draw your fake guns, cowboy,
                         and splash your fake blood

                across the fake world
                of your profitable screens
                but let my people go
                free and gentle.
                Life is not a movie
                except for minds
                that move in darkness.
                Winter belongs to them
                but spring is ours.

At noon the sun foreshadows summer, though the wild
rabbits are still white as snow. A pair of robins
bent already on breeding, pick for precocious worms
among the stiff and wilted grass. A squirrel searches
the spruce tree half a century high for the first sign
of sprouting among early grosbeaks and warblers.

                This is the month when the light
                tilts the balance of time in
                favour of life. Mornings are
                brutal to those caught
                in the inertia of night.
                We must take sides
                with the season. Winter is never
                more than a tropopause away.

A grey wall moves across
the afternoon, pushes the blue
sky beyond all horizons,
crumbles in a sudden gust
of wind and flakes into
a million bits and pieces
of textured ice—a blizzard
settles its rigid symmetry
on the just awakening fields
and forests. The storm-ruffled
birds huddle in the dark
interior of a clump of cedars
that never surrender
their green to any season.
Beware. March is as two-faced
as its god and
brings woe to all
who have no shelter.

        More vicious than a winter storm
        in spring they came
        to Cabañas province: police
        and soldiers trained at Fort Bragg.
        Rosita was tied up and forced
        to watch. They scraped
        the skin from her father's
        face, chopped off his fingers
        one by one, pushed a rifle up
        his rectum and fired. Rosita
        watched and her six years stretched
        into a century of pain.
        Her screams shook a flock
        of zopilotes from a nearby tree
        like black rotting fruit.

In the spring earth bulbs stir
and jostle the dark. Sap sickers
up beneath bark, triggering
a synthesis of light. The three
hundred million suns of Andromeda
are a puff of snow in the black
branches of outer space. Crows wheel
about the weeping willow by the creek
that rushes iceshards to a green
ceremony. Suddenly the chill air
is fractured by a scream—

        The soldiers stripped her mother
        raped her one by one, then sliced
        open her belly, tore out the seven-
        months old foetus and chopped it up
        before throwing it to the dogs to eat.
        Rosita watched, her horror had long
        become a stone that choked all sense
        and sensibility from her just awakening
        mind, her eyes rigid, still seeing
        from her severed head a swarm of flies
        circling into her throat, black stars dancing
        a season of blood on her retina, the last
        image faltering quickly fading into the
        darksweet smell of her childish, eternal night.

Blind man, where are you
taking us? Is this
the promised land
of your fine books
and speeches?
How far is it
to the visions
of Mozart and Neruda,
Walt Whitman and van Gogh?

                        Cry, my beloved,
                      we've lost our way.
              The stars are rushing off
                in all directions
              at the speed of light,
              but we must stay
      alone in this winter wasteland
        of interstellar space where
           spring is but a brief
              interlude. The end
              of the world is more
            than eighteen billion
              light years away
            but we can reach it
      in one generation because
        the future is embedded
        in the brain's hemispheres –
between the hemispheres of power
        and of comprehension
               right and left
           of language and being:
            the choice is spring.

The buds in their hard shells survived the last blizzard.
The icy night that laid siege to the living withdraws
at dawn. Rock elm and jackpine stretch into the early
light. A flock of wild geese puts a check mark against
the sky where the sun crosses the celestial equator.

                                        Wake up, blind man!
                                        The light comes naked
                                        to the living.

Lakes fissure as ice turns into rivers that overflow
their banks and swiftly wash away the stains of winter.

                                        The March sun sends us
                                        trillions of calories
                                        every second to feed
                                        the multitudes of creatures
                                        on this green planet.

Where the red-eyed goshawk swoops down the updrift slopes of
spring, a beaver dives into the cold current that murmured
tales of green trembling aspen all through its long sleep.

                                        A hundred billion neurons
                                        are sending signals charged
                                        via a hundred trillion synapses
                                        to connect past and future
                                        to the incomprehensible.

Mornings shake off the lethargy of hibernation and leap
into consciousness with the shrill cries of bluejays.
Woodpeckers knock frantically on the windows of perception.

                                        The poor will no longer
                                        starve to death for us.
                                        El hambre del pueblo
                                        es la culpa del gobierno.
                                        Send your soldiers home!

This is the month that falls
into the arms of Venus,
the goddess Mars took
for all that is gentle and free.

                                        We cannot escape spring.
                                        The redshift in the heart
                                        measures the distance
                                        we have travelled from
                                        our humanity. Dawn flows

like blood into Rosita's
rigid eyes where everything
is renewed from the roots
and night grows young again.

2. April Fools

And the sun is young again
running halfway through the constellation
of the Ram leaping from planet
to planet spending its energies
in explosive abandon as though
five billion years were an eternity
speeding dawn faster than a bullet
through silences as ancient as asteroids
crossing darkly timeless skies
to throw himself into the arms of
spruce and pine, aspen and ash
their green hands pulling the light
close lowering it radiantly to
the ground whispering that spring
has arrived on the lips of a warm
wind promising us the dance of our lives.

                                      The light cannot stand still.
                                      It comes in waves breaking on
                                      surfaces into a spectacle of
                                      colours bouncing from rock to
                                      leaf to skin and back again
                                      into the eye: on the mind's
                                      black screen movement shapes
                                      colours move shapes move into
                                      sounds move mind shapes
                                      images into words
                                      into knowing
                                      seeing—

a yellowshafted flicker drills
for grubs beneath the bark
of a dying elm, punctures
the membrane of dreams
and lets the morning break
flicker-flicker into consciousness.

                                      Spring is here.
                                      Nothing stands still.
                                      Winter is but a mask
                                      on the face of the river

                                        that runs on beyond
                                        the end of my song.
                                        In the subatomic theatre
                                        a dialectic of particles
                                        and energies reforms regroups
                                        reconnects electrons pro-
                                        tons neutrons at systematic
                                        random to tease the senses
                                        into a feast of familiar
                                        images. Other molecules other
                                        rhythms other appearances:
                                        the season choreographs spring
                                        for a classical performance.

Delicate
and smooth the blue
grey hands of the cohosh
reach from the rot of winter holding
half hiding its palmful of greenish yellow
flowers like the pale hands of a sage sheltering
tiny flames of truth in a wildflower temple, its papoose
root prepared to ease the birth of children. Up north cotton grass
drives its green spikes through recalcitrant snow to stake the claims
of bogs and wave a bright plume from each tall blade defiant as a cat's paw.
The prairie crocus grows fur against the arctic wind shudders
and blooms, casting out the cold with a spell of blossoms,
a pale mauve veil across the naked earth while deep
inside the moisture-laden shades of forests
Jack stands stiff and purple in his pulpit
to proclaim a speechless ecstasy.
Creeks and rivers, swollen
as veins in a rush of
passion, flood
their banks
discharge
snow
melt
and
ice
crush into a million lakes in time into the salt sea.

A rage born
in the primal oceans
obsesses the dance
flowers and rivers
sing to the sea
with the same fury
that drives beasts
to prey. Spring
leaves a trail
of blood
up and down
paths of renewal
the mind must journey
on pain of death
to reach fulfillment.
From the burning
centre of earth
El Chichón spits
in the sky's face
and spreads
volcanic ash
to suffocate
a northern summer.
Free energies move
in all directions
like free minds.
Are you ready
for spring
to make love
the temper of
the new light?

The sweet showers of April
have turned to acid rain
and Zephirus' fragrant breath
is laced with nitrogen and sulphur
corroding the young and tender
shoots corroding our lungs
the very stones corroding
what we believe in. Our lakes
are dying pike and bass
duckweed and water
lily poisoned from
the smokestacks
of the makers
and takers
of money.

        Fools
        mistake greenbacks
        for a sign of spring.
        All that is tender
        about money is that
        it is legal. Ask
        your local panhandler.
        The blind leading
        the deaf by the
        purse. It's all been
        said before: money is
        power is war is death.
        Still we listen
        to the promises
        money makes. Have you
        ever listened to
        the promises it keeps?—
        the boy soldier
        legs shot off yelling
        for his mother as he
        bleeds his life into
        foreign soil shellshocked
        his patriotism fouls
        his pants too late
        for him to be true
        to himself. Or the seal
        mother wailing on

an ice floe as they
peel her pup with
skillful knife like a
ripe furry fruit. Try
to sell suffering
in the free market or
to purchase happiness.

Have you ever heard
the hoarse voice of
hunger coming cracked
and tearless from a
bloated belly putrid
as a bubble of swamp
gas? Rent compassion
for a day and see
the world on an open
installment plan.
Invest your feelings
in spring shares
of the mind and watch
yourself grow
into the universe.

Along eastern roads a million tiny suns
are bursting into coltsfoot flowers
and Indian thistles have lit their scarlet
flames out west in bracts of lace.
The woods are heavy and tumescent
with moisture, mist drifts and hangs drops
of water in bare branches where each swells
and trembles with the tiny foetus of a quickening
world upside down before it falls and shatters
delivering life to roots and tubers. Rain has painted
the tree trunks black sombre palisades against
a larger vision through the dew's prism.
The ground has thawed now
though patches of snow still cling
to shadows and cool their dark blood.
Everywhere the sap is running
to the light, the fields
breathe faster, lakes
stir with spawn and

tadpole, the forest talks
in many tongues
of birth and breeding
as the sun makes winter's dreams
come true, fusing past
and future in the welding
arc of its photosphere.
It takes five million tons
of hydrogen per second
to burn a hole
into the black impalpable
ice of interplanetary space
large enough for a world
to green for spring to
happen is a process
is an unfolding of autumn's
unfinished designs into summer's
commitments. There are
no beginnings
and no endings,
only transformations.

                                             This is the month of many
                                             longings. Every birth wakes
                                             echoes of a primal scream
                                             at the light. The dark of death
                                             dazzles pilgrims and lures
                                             them to distant shores
                                             in search of resurrections.
                                             But they sit in their
                                             cameras turning a blind
                                             eye to the mind's exposures.

City of the Jebusites: you left your doors
open and the blind and the lame entered.
They came on camelback, marauding Habiru tribes,
to take your homes and your lives, god's dagger-happy
savages, to destroy your faith in sky and sea,
sun and earth, and claim your city as a gift
from heaven. But the angels had their throats
cut by the swords of pharaohs, caesars, caliphs,
and kings, drawing a circle of blood in the desert
where your walls stand in the name of many gods.

How shall we ever be at home among souvenir shops
where a procession of fools winds its dolorous way
through the year 1982, prostrates itself in rows
of turbans before an ancient rock in the year 1402,
then segregates before a limestone wall into queues
of men and women wailing over the year 5742? *Al Quds*.
So much devotion and so little that is holy. Except
for the three holy fools who preached crusades and *jihads*
in the name of peace, each claiming the light and the truth
that belong to no one. But darkness cannot be blinded or banished.

                                    Born in a barn, drifting
                                    among bulrushes, or herding
                                    sheep, a child is a child
                                    of its time, each the centre
                                    of a universe that has
                                    no centre. Darkness is always
                                    on the face of the deep
                                    and in the beginning there was
                                    no beginning, only the eternal
                                    return of the same
                                    particles to the same cosmic
                                    implosion exploding
                                    as though space were breathing
                                    fire and inhaling light,
                                    each breath lasting thirty
                                    billion years. What remains
                                    is brooding in silence.

And the procession moves on under a spreading
cloud of volcanic ash carrying the torch
of folly through the museum of three faiths
mumbling muttering to ancient stones, Holy
Friday under the Dome of the Rock, Pesach
Shabbat along the Wailing Wall, Easter
Sunday by the Rock of the Skull—their prayer

                                    shattered by a good man be-
                                    lieving on the Temple Mount
                                    with an M-16 automatic
                                    killing because he had to
                                    because the Pentateuch
                                    because Abraham Moses

                              and Mohammed because all
                              the prophets and redeemers
                              with their sacred deadly logic:

always God's children must defend the indefensible
almighty commanding armies of worshippers piously
wading through the millennia knee-deep in blood
spilled by infidels by the faithful by the book
the revengeful Torah the puritanical New Testament
the fanatical suras—oh the gruesome tectonics of dogmas
clashing like continents crushing all in their paths
subducting our humanity and raising hues and cries!
And still the nations charter their rights and freedoms
to the supremacy of a god whose wars are holy.

                              City of belfries and cupolas, spires
                              and minarets, hold back the desert
                              as your walls have done since
                              before the biblical onslaught.
                              You don't belong to prophets
                              or to prophecies. Nor to fools
                              who make of their brains, hearts
                              and souls sacred stones. Cross
                              a star with a crescent moon and
                              you get an eclipse of the mind
                              where holy asses climb farting
                              to their respective heavens
                              leaving you nothing
                              but turds—a feast
                              for devout beetles
                              and pious scavengers.
                              Disciples are the executioners
                              of what they don't understand.
                              They make the mystery
                              of being a power
                              play and turn love
                              to shares and bonds
                              of a different kind.
                              Wake up, fools of the faiths!
                              Time has moved beyond belief.
                              Spring is here to stay
                              winter's machinations.

Plant bitter herbs
for the slavery of all
people. Drink salt water
for the tears of suffering
everywhere. Bells toll
like hearts of bronze
blunting the mind's
passions, and *muezzins*
wail *salaam* from minarets
to put holy blinkers
on the inner eye.

                                            All around us
                                            spacetime
                                            unfolds
                                            four dimensions
                                            inside us.

Under the delicate
dome of every egg
the code for creation
unscrambles itself.
Every cell carries
fire and water air
and earth forward
generation by
generation closer
to freedom. Imperfect
shelter of almost
perfection where
the cellular knots
are tied that bind
ash and breath into
a garland of nature.
Behold the fowls of the air. They feed themselves
                                            but wordless their wings
                                            are a blessing
                                            of mystery. Consider
                                            the lilies in the field.
                                            Their roots toil
                                            in darkness, but the
                                            synagogues of their flowers
                                            are full of praise. Watch

                              the salmon's pilgrimage
                              upstream to the stained glass
                              chapel of the river's
                              source to triumph over
                              their dying. The hills kneel
                              at the foot of mountains
                              to grace the light
                              under a blue canopy
                              in the grand mosque
                              of the sky. And Allah
                              is absolute
                              emptiness: intergalactic
                              space bound to meaning
                              by the neural chains
                              in the skull only
                              where the cortex
                              forges our world
                              sees it as though

it had a heart of gold
(not the fool's gold of makers
and takers of money, that paperthin
passion of wilted lives)—our heart
blazes like the sacred metal of the ancients
who knew the sun
giveth and taketh
heat rain breath spring
the wind whispering the trembling of a leaf the lake's
lapping at the shore the spasm in the loin an eye
blinking the flash of an idea striking. Every flicker
                              of life or matter is a tiny
                              flame blasted from the sun's
                              nuclear furnace across
                              a hundred million miles
                              of absolute winter
                              to make patterns here
                              to delight and torture
                              its own gesturing.

The sun reflects in a million dewdrops
and burns its energies methodically
in the veins and ventricles of every
flower every tree beast river or thought.

                    Fifteen million degrees of heat
                    raging at the core through
                    absorption screens and convection
                    filters, torn between gravitation
                    and explosion, each gamma ray
                    travels ten million years layer
                    by fiery layer to reach the sun's
                    blackbody spectrum and pass through
                    its photosphere for a swift leap
                    into visibility here
                    to be converted into
                    the temperature of blood.

Is there not ecstasy enough
in this perpetual holocaust of creation
for a love to encompass all?
Billions of heartbeats drumming
spring into consciousness, each one driven
by a tiny flame flickering between fear
and desire. All creation is transformation.
Between ice and fire a moment
of flowering rarer and more precious
in the rarified spheres around stars and
galaxies than emeralds in a nightmare
of burning pitch. Or is gold
the sun's pool of tears
wept over human folly? Oh if
the stars could cry the heavens
would turn into a salt sea!

                    On this planet of plenty
                    four hundred million
                    children go to bed
                    hungry every night
                    and more than one
                    million of them
                    will starve to death
                    in this month of
                    flowers and rebirth.
                    Skin sagging on thin bones,
                    belly ballooning, eyes big
                    and protruding, fifty children
                    die on every page of poetry

you read. Images for corpses.
Is this price fixed
for every song
in heaven or on earth?
Allahu Akhabar. In the holy
land a godblind people
sacrifice children to a tribal
urge. Humpty-Dumpty sat
on a wall. When a bullet
punctured the belly of
a seven-year old boy.
Humpty-Dumpty had a great
fall. In the bullet-shattered
brain of a five-year old
girl. And all the world's
money and all the world's
gods cannot put either
together again. Humpty-Dumpty
of the universe, you stand up
neither to rhyme nor reason
with your lame horses and
your blind men forever
locked into your nursery
of diabolical fire and
brimstone games surrounded
by all your childish celestial toys.

I have climbed out
the window of my eyes
on to the earth to plant
a garden down the years
and walk the limits
of my freedom, followed
by Rosita's rigid eyes
that stare out to sea now
where a procession of gunships
have embarked under a circling
cloud of El Chichón's ash on a
pilgrimage to the god whose shrine
holds the wretched relics
of power: scraps of flesh
splinters of bone shreds of
brain mutilations amputations—

                such is honour among nations.
                No sickness to be healed
                by this martyrdom of fools
                that inflicts blindness on all
                sober men and true who
                bring offerings of missiles and torpedoes
                and the gift of their infuriated pride
                down south to the other pole
                where the underprivileged are frenzied
                by the privilege of giving their lives
                for the god and country of their generals
                sailing the ocean blue
                flying the sky grey
                back to a winter of the heart.

Bloodroots rise from rich woodland
soil simmering acrid juice that once dyed
Indian faces red for war, puccoons opening
their petals to the sun's hot push only.
Deep in the forest's dark fornices the milk
of mammals flows softly—a warm river
raising countless cubs to consciousness.
Fur stalks and strikes to feed new
generations while hidden in their nests
eggs hatch in a fluff and flurry of feathers
beating the air for breath calling for life
worms and flies to catch a birdsong.
Rabbits molt and mount among the pines.

                Though blizzards still
                have their moments
                deep in the south
                of this spring, April
                is the month the earth
                fills its cup up north
                with rain and drinks
                a toast to the season
                engendering a passion
                between Mars and Venus
                that is our destiny.
                Between them our tolerance
                is a few degrees of blood—
                the thin wedge
                of a thousand fables.

This is the month
light lures what is
dark from hiding.
Fools fall into the trap
of their own gullibility.
We are perishable
cousins of the stones
and of the clouds
spinning between stars.
What remains is of spring
is what is here true
where the blue-eyed grass
blooms once around the clock
here in spacetime where
the sun and the mind
and between them

                      a song now
                  and then a search
                  unfold dancing.

3. May Song and Dance

A sweet song is unfolding
about Jack-in-the Green.
Pretty maidens are weaving
a garland for their queen.
For May is here,
the birds appear
to celebrate a feast of light
while lovers are dancing
each dawn into the night.

                    I hear a childhood
                    soprano drifting
                    down the river
                    of my years
                    carrying a tune
                    across the improbable
                    chaos of subatomic
                    worlds where photons
                    leptons mesons baryons
                    seek random partners
                    in quintillionths of
                    a second, form
                    and reform chains
                    in the waltzing
                    rock and roll time
                    of quantum space,
                    dancing us
                    into and out of
                    the light by the dark
                    forces of waves
                    that are not
                    waves. Believe it

or not, my beloved, you are
awake, we are awake, they
are awake who compose
models and write scenarios
that belong to a dream—
you and I dancing close
with stars and electrons

to the strains of a memory
that holds us together
as tenaciously as the web
the spider's world. Any
remembrance threads
random events into a life.
You and I are more improbable
than a miracle, knotting
moment to moment crisscross
a net to catch the meaning of a star.

                                        Out across the Atlantic
                                        Venus rises mounts
                                        rides the dark stallion
                                        with his mane of spume
                                        flying from the velvet swell
                                        the muscle-straining sea
                                        between her bright thighs
                                        till the sun rushes
                                        its blood into the sky
                                        and she disappears
                                        in a cloud of stardust.

Once upon many legends they built her
temples as votives for victory in war.
The pillars were trees about a sacred
grove where knights pledged eternal love
on their swords and ladies disdained
to be their sheaths. The amorous raised
dying to the pitch of loving as they
danced fields and forests into grace
danced children into heaven
till myths became astronomy that left
the tender goddess burning in the sky
sixty-seven million miles from the sun
that rises in the West for her.

                                        We have sung your beauty
                                        down the ages, Venus,
                                        not knowing your blond
                                        hair was but a hurricane
                                        of sulphuric acid
                                        and your fair eyes

                              were volcanoes. You barely
                              move under your layers
                              and layers of carbon
                              dioxide, though your blistering
                              passion would crush
                              our bones. Sibling planet,
                              are you holding up a mirror
                              to our different fate
                              or to our future?
                              Your hothouse tomb
                              is our green pantheon.
                              Are we turning the heat too high?

The young trees are unfurling
their first leaves in the wind
and the fragrance of flowers
makes all our senses sing.
For May is here
for us to cheer
the honeymoon of earth and sun.
Burn the puppets of winter,
our loving has begun.

                              Sing along, soldier, while
                              you can. You'll be called up
                              and away from the ceremonies
                              of your youth to play
                              macabre games
                              far from home.

                              Bullets thunder down barrels
                              triggering a shrill carnival
                              of blood and pain
                              that ends the seasons
                              of youth in a wheel
                              chair or a grave.
                              Guns talk
                              with glottal stops.

Village streets dance through valleys
of flowers where boys and girls bring May
home with branches and garlands round
and round the pole in the green and red

of their folklore: Robin Hood and Will Scarlet
their hearts full of the valour of love,
Tom piping and the Fool ringing his bells—
music that beats no march but may sing
a milky maiden to the sky, Morris dance
to cast out the demons of winter,
a straw puppet burning in the soul.

                              The early wind still
                              tastes faintly of snow
                              though it smells of fire.
                              The aspens shudder.
                              Spiders dance in the cool
                              silk of dawn, stringing
                              their nets across the mouth
                              of morning. Some hang heavy
                              with a catch of dew
                              swinging softly in the soaring
                              grasses. On the coast
                              fishermen knot webs
                              into ocean currents
                              for the herring run

while far out among the foam-flecked
horses of the sea a grim song
and dance of warships moves south through
the fog of their own pomp and circumstance
past the dark sockets that once sparkled
with Rosita's young eyes filled now
with earth and worms and a half-burnt match.

                              Sober men and true
                              destroyers sailing cruisers
                              down the ocean blue
                              submarines attentive to their
                              aircraft carriers duty
                              delivering yesterday's pride
                              of troops and cannons
                              aboard the saucy beauty
                              of their invincible frigates
                              halfway around a world
                              of satellites and radar
                              to the heroes on tomorrow's
                              sobering battlefield:

a scattering of rocks
that goaded a macho junta
duped a proud people
to hail an act of piracy
as a point of honour.
Slow dance of *abuelas*
in the Plaza de Mayo
holding hands with ten
thousand *desaparecidos*
across mass graves
where mutilated flesh
rots with the gruesome
tales of generals and butchers
that root in blood
and sprout phallic flowers
in a garden of gore
where the scythe-and-bone
man dances a jig.

                        Is this the way
                        to celebrate spring
                        or summer when
                        every dance is praise,
                        when every dance says
                        Yes—except
                        the dance of guns and
                        knives in the gut?

You and I are
a wild unlikely dance
of particles moving
to a music so delicate
a cough could end it,
a flicker not to be
perceived in the circles
of galaxies. Andromeda is
wheeling a hundred thousand
centuries of light towards us
at the speed of fifty miles
per second, but the sun will burn
the earth to cinders before
our sister galaxy arrives
to find no trace of us.

A fool meets the challenge
of this universe as a hero.

*We are all together
at a place
I cannot disclose,
with a great deal of arms
I cannot detail,
ready for an objective
I cannot reveal—*
said the mustachioed officer
to inform the public
of the current state
of military
metaphysics.

Pick your branches of hawthorn,
of sycamore and ash.
Put a blessing on lovers,
their spirit and their flesh.
For May is here,
what do you fear
when summer sings in every heart?
Tonight if our love is true
we do not have to part.

The village band plays
and boys pick their girls
who have already picked
their boys in the wishing-well
of their dreams with garlands
of flowers in their hair.
Aboard ship a navy band plays
a different tune and death
has already picked its boys.
Oh, better to live and die
under the brave flag we fly!
A princely fleet of sober
men and true has sailed below
the tropic of winter and
reached its destination:
a handful of grey rocks
in grey waters under grey skies.

They didn't choose the place
nor pick the weapons,
who came to slap a general's
and save a lady's face
and died to get satisfaction.
An armada sent for a courtly
joust turned technological, a naval
show of force turned bloody
on invaders who could not bear
the thought of half a million foreign
sheep. Democracy? A handful
of glittering dust to flatter fools.
Vanity is the tomb of reason. Was ever
war fought for more? Or less?
Long marches of death and devastation
from Xenophon to Mao, Bolivar
to Napoleon, Hannibal to Hitler, footsore
and battle-fatigued men have blazed
trails of blood across this planet
on land and water and in the air,
always for the good of man-
kind, and still man is no kinder
than the good he finds in himself.
How many corpses does an abstraction weigh?

                                                  An idiot is counting
                                                  the stars
                                                  dancing on the waves
                                                  like water lilies
                                                  in the wake
                                                  of sombre ships.

Desolate islands in the rain
in the wind in the ceaseless
rain in the cold wind surf—
lashing bare rocks in the hard
spray in the grey salt-saturated
rain winds to whom they belong.
Penguins are at home here, bowing
like sanctimonious humans
to visitors and invaders
with equal indifference.
There are no trees to raise

a fist against the fierce
antarctic storms. A black-browed
albatross calls among the sooty
shearwaters and ground-tyrants.
One nation's Falklands are
another nation's Malvinas.

                                  This the month
                                  Napoleon was born
                                  and Voltaire died
                                  and the lilies of the valley
                                  listened to St. Francis.
                                  In the ribbed vaults
                                  of maples and beeches
                                  the morning star has
                                  dissolved into options.
                                  The birds know
                                  you can trust
                                  trees.
                                  They point
                                  to the stars
                                  they can never
                                  reach.

Let us join hands and dance round
this gaily festooned tree.
We are burying winter,
the sun has set us free.
For May is here
to wake the year
from sleep as deep and dark as death.
We rejoice now in springtime
when all things draw new breath.

                       In the month of leafage
                       light assumes the sweet
                       taste of life. Underground
                       the arteries of darkness
                       swell. Hairy roots and lateral
                       roots, tap roots and root
                       tips soak seep fill with
                       force sap into columns up
                       by cohesion and pressure

through the tubes and spindles
of the xylem into the green
honeycomb chambers of the
mesophyll where trees trade
oxygen for carbon with
the accommodating air.
For three hundred million
years pine and spruce have
brought the dark to light
and breathed life into flesh
and blood from pole to
pole. Dinosaurs have come
and gone since angiosperms
have greened and flowered
in a synthesis of sun
and sap. Heartwood darkens
at the core as cambium
cells divide into bast
under the bark wrinkling
with age.

Elms are ripening
their seeds on yellow
green wings as the
first leaves break
obliquely from pink
bud scales. Oaks
and beeches are hanging
their tasseled catkins
into the wind
scattering their gold
among the young
emerald leaves.
At the shoot tips
of spruce trees
crimson female flowers
open delicately
to the drift of pollen.

Down south, alas, May
has arrived with guns
blazing into winter.
Below all latitudes

of reason the sea turns
crimson with burning
ships and sailors' blood.
Missiles and torpedoes
blow the mind
with gashing wounds
and sinking courage
the salt burning the sea
strangling the young
bleeding better than
any flag, ship or
shattering victory.

Sacred trees,
sanctuary of birds
and ancient spirits,
that hold heaven
and earth together
in the green cycle
of fire and water.
I heard a hermit
thrush sing
at daybreak
clear as a flute
in a hemlock tree.

Forlorn archipelago
without trees, without
significance in the calendars
of power except to a distant
pride, the winds of war now
press you like a brand seal
into the sea's flesh
to sear an arcadian memory
forever. The surf hisses as rock
bites into waves as bullets
bite into flesh and bone
attackers and defenders taste
the smell of blood.

No warning. A high pitch
hits you roaring a punch
in the stomach. Stunning.

No pain. Just fear. Sweetness
fills the mouth. You wonder
at your sticky hands. A warm
trickle down the chin. "Time
to get up for school." Crimson
stain on mother's dressing-
gown. Ketchup. Blood. *Mother,
I don't want to...*—Blackness
falls into eyes like a stone.
You hear a gasp—your own!
A metallic rigour spreads. Pain.
Your mouth gushes. Panic. Vomit.
Please. I can't breathe... Puta madre! My belly. Damn you all!

                              Fighter-bomber pilots never
                              see their victims. They
                              cut the screaming air
                              into heroic patterns looping
                              the light through the thrill
                              of death, leaving a trail
                              of blood in the sky. Listen
                              when the guns are silent.

Our round dance continues
to orbit in the sky.
At the hub of the seasons
the greening pole stands high.
For May is here,
the light is sheer
and weaves the flowers into spring
on the loom of our loving
the whole world comes to sing.

                              Exocet missiles tigerfish
                              torpedoes sea-king helicopters
                              skyhawks mirages blowpipe
                              rockets and scorpion tanks—
                              I have the spilled blood
                              of soldiers in my pen.
                              They went into battle
                              with a song in their mouths
                              before the guns led them
                              a mad dance to end all

                                            dancing. Was there no
                                            one to tell them that
                                            the neocortex is the seat
                                            of reason and that it evolved
                                            from the limbic system of love?

What matters is spread
across a hundred billion galaxies
among a hundred billion times
as many stars, each a holocaust
streaking through a wasteland
that cares no more for you and me
than for a scattering of rocks
in the sea. There is peace only
when there is nothing. In the nuclear
furnace of each sun particles
forge the logic that must lead
to life. The DNA is as inevitable
as the universe. Are we, then, part
of the rhetoric of stars? And is war
the logical conclusion of an absurd
proposition? Everything is possible, except—

                                            Failure, says her Majesty,
                                            who knows all about it,
                                            is impossible.—I have
                                            the spilled blood of my
                                            soldiers on my back,
                                            answers the general.
                                            Queen Elaine and Sir Galahad
                                            who once moved troubadours
                                            to song inspire carnage here
                                            for pride is now a virtue.

May dances have turned into parades
where boys and girls wear uniforms
and carry guns in place of branches.
The garlands in their hair
are helmets now and flowers
are awarded as medals
for the courage to deny
the logic of the heart.

                              This is peacetime. There
                              is faith yet. In holy land
                              an unholy army is waiting
                              for a pretext to devastate
                              a neighbour whom they
                              love. There is hope
                              yet. The marines are ready
                              to save El Salvador
                              for the Banco Hispanamericano.
                              There is charity yet. In Poland
                              troops have taken up
                              water cannons to silence
                              solidarity. Give unto
                              Caesar. A minimum of
                              three wars a year
                              is needed to maintain
                              peace. Over a hundred
                              wars since the second world
                              holocaust. The future
                              is bright. There are enough
                              nuclear weapons for a
                              spectacular
                              curtain so that the fool
                              can take a bow
                              wiping strontium ninety
                              from his make-up
                              brow. There's no one
                              left to applaud.

The sun rages through the constellation
of the bull between whose horns
a star exploded and collapsed
into a neutron core till a grain
weighed a million tons.
And still the Crab Nebula
expands at six hundred miles
a second hurling the wreckage
of all that was possible
all order and achievement
into the black limbo of space.

                              Those who are awake
                              can see

                                    the cosmos
                                    is one
                                    infinite
                                    round
                                    of catastrophes.
                                    All that is
                                    gentle and free
                                    grows in the gardens
                                    of our eyes.
                                    A little closer
                                    to the sun
                                    the light turns black,
                                    a little farther away
                                    the night goes blind.

The elm trees are building
fan vaults to support the sky,
their green tracery a ritual
to bless the house. Grosbeaks
and bluejays, waxwings and killdeer
call their echo in the cloisters
of the bush. Behind the stained glass
window of a lake someone is hoisting
the sun into place. The filigree shadow
of cedars patterns a last patch
of great white trilliums where
in the hollow of a dead butternut
raccoons raise their young. Under
the weeping arches of willows lovers
hold the future of a planet in their arms.
Their intimacies are fulfilled in the asymmetry
of leaves, each as unique and perishable
as the stars dancing and our hearts singing
in the green solitude between quasars
and quarks where all flesh is as the grass
and mind a passion of pulsating light.

Summer: The Devil's Club

4. Where Shall the Birds Fly?

> *Where can we go on crossing this last border?*
> *Where do birds fly after the final sky?*
> *Where do plants sleep when all the winds have passed?*
> *We write our names in coloured smoke*
> *and we die in this final passage*
> *that olive trees might grow*
> *to mark our place.*
> Mahmoud Darweesh, *Earth Narrows Before Us*

Everywhere the grass is ravishing
the earth, its roots penetrating the dark
to fetch it into the green morning
where a wind warm as blood blows
the light gently into summer's mouth.
Shadows shrink towards the sun
and at its zenith the mind
must measure its own mystery
against the passionate flesh.

        The apple trees are suffering
    their June drop: fruit flawed perhaps
    aborts, the grassgreen matted finish
      beads falling, the rags of wilted
      blossoms still attached to them
     like crippled wings. In the crotch
      of cherry branches tent caterpillars
  spin sheets of webbing into layered
transparencies from which they crawl
     in languid processions to forage
      on young leaves. Silk passage
    to the veiled rites of pupation.
    Butterflies and moths. A fly catcher
    balances on a power line by flip
   of tail, surveys the morning's buzz
and hum, then tumbles to a swift dive
  to reave bug or beetle from the air.

           This is the month Hermes rules,
          god of thieves and merchants,
             messenger of the gods:

what's the news on high?
The rich are robbing you blind
because there's more money
in bullets than in bread
and they've turned the rains now
into vinegar at the stock market
so they can trade the blue
right out of the sky before you
can paint it the colour of blood.

Tell every broker
the stars are not
for sale. Ask them:
Where shall the birds fly
after the final sky?

Arid and breathless, Mercury runs
ellipses round the sun, hugging
its orbit so close that lead melts
at the height of day while its one night
a year is cold enough to liquefy air.
For aeons the heavens cratered
the first planet, each asteroid strike
gouging its face till it was battered
into another lunar wasteland.

But for the relentless wind and the grinding waters,
but for the frost's crowbar and the crunch of continents,
but for the laser sun and the solvents of life,
the alchemy of trees and the slow flameless fire
in the guts of beasts our blue planet too
would stare at space with the empty eyes
and the savaged face of a violent past
recording a billion-year bombardment, the brutal
expression of a sky forever bent on catastrophe.

The universe conceals
its chaos from us
by strategies it programs
into our retina, turning
nuclear holocausts
into ceremonies of gods
and music, mathematics

          and colour—until once more
              a meteor strikes
              and buries life's
            most daring travellers
         in a millennium of winters.

Summer solstice is close enough
now for a hatching of ant eggs.
Already the devil's paintbrush
is putting orange touches
to the blue air, and black
leaf beetle larvae are gnawing
away the underside of cottonwood
leaves till only the skeletons
of veins are left trembling
on this young season's breath.

          And I am condemned to wander
           through these woods and fields
            backpacking the skeletons
             of my childhood. Between
         buttercups brimful with golden
           light and the plaintive call
       of catbirds, over the reed-bending
       pond, behind the secretive gestures
       of trees, memories hover in search
            of a final resting-place.

              The smell of burning cities, burning flesh
           overpowers the pine-scented breeze. I smell fear
              and in among aspen leaves I see glittering
            stains, always in pairs, small discs shimmering
           ovals of light: glasses spectacles frames twisted
          pince-nez entangled a whole mound of eye-glasses
           shattered blind reflecting askew a cracked sun
           burning holes in cedar shadows where eyes full of
             pain and terror, whole galaxies of eyes large
           with fear glow like foxfire in a cankered world.

     Behind a Bach concert
    in the mind's crimped folds
      an evil magic flips
   the familiar into a flush

>of horror, turning each wood
>stand muscular with beeches
>into Buchenwald, recalling
>the victims in the bluejay's
>screeches, and conjuring up
>a whole summer full of death
>camps for boys and girls.

I hear the howls of men and women
hung from dislocated limbs, swinging
jerking in their sockets I hear shots
bullets thud screaming into flesh
scrupulous not to kill too soon:

>Stand to attention,
>*Schweinhunde!*
>That's what happens
>when you displease
>authority power pride
>with your convictions
>your looks your being
>different your genes.
>Sing, *Judenlümmel,*
>sing for your life!
>All we want is your
>watches your gold
>teeth your dignity.

Wir werden weitermarschieren…
>Is it true is it true
>that we'll march on and on…

bis alles in Scherben fällt…
>till all the world lies in ruins…

und morgen die ganze Welt…
>till you and I
>are but a charcoal impression
>in a future rock formation?

          Where do the twisted trees of hatred grow?
             In what polluted soil of the heart?
              Is it the acid rain of injustice,
                the lethal monoxides of fear
                 or the pesticides of greed
                     that nurture them?
                  Does someone else's pain
                    teach no lessons? What
                       about your own?

           My memories roar with the fire
           storms of Hamburg and Dresden,
          linger acrid in the smouldering ruins
           of Leningrad and Stalingrad, smell
           the macabre sweetness of the smoke
              over Birkenau and Belsen
               and now smoke billows
              over the cities of the Levant:

O Sidon, jewel of Phoenician cities,
you traded the treasures of the earth
and of the sea, your bazaars bargained
for the envy of kings and queens
farther back than Babylon. Homer
sang the praises of your artisans
but he knew wealth and beauty
are the undoing of men and women
cities and empires: something
craves to destroy what it cannot
possess. You were laid to ashes
by the Philistines and reborn
from the same stone, turned to ruins
by Mongols and by Moslems rebuilt
you were ruled ravaged and restored
by Assyrians Persians Egyptians
Romans Arabs Franks and Ottomans
in the ceaseless tides of history
till now your ancient walls
must endure once more
fire and force of invaders.

                                        Not to dust do we turn
                                        but to ashes. Everything
                                        will burn to ashes.
                                        Everything is born from ashes,
                                        even the inconceivable void
                                        after the final sky.
                                        In another thirty-five sun years
                                        the earth will be a sea
                                        of boiling lava, as our star
                                        burns up its last hydrogen
                                        preparing for the helium flash
                                        that will light the slow fuse
                                        of the final solar pyrotechnics
                                        leaving it a white dwarf
                                        blazing inexorably to cinders.
              So the heart is
              a fire the sun
              ignites in the dark
              of carbohydrate tempests
              burning us up
              in all the colours
              the spectrum can mix
              between a blinding red
              giant and a fugitive
              black hole. Solar
              flames became flesh
              became song in the blood
              crucible where life
              is freed from slag
              and dross to be cast
              in the delicate shapes
              and patterns of dances,
              images, words. Time
              in its round-the-clock
              laboratory distilled
              amino acids into algae,
              arthropods, chordates
              and worms, each burning
              to consume other fires
              or be consumed by them
              in the advance of living
              flames—fish, insects, reptiles,
              birds and mammals, till

        neurons fired in the flesh
       its one saving grace: love—
and survival became a ceremony
          not a victory:

                                       I love
                                therefore I am
                                    human.

At summer solstice we used to celebrate
life's pyrotechnics with fireworks of our own:
a giant wheel was rolled flaming into the river
and the night exploded with seedballs of red
shooting-stars and golden rainstorms raging
over song-laden boats and our harmonica
and bonfire hearts dancing garlands of flowers
into a sweeter future. But the cross
that crooked its arms at right angles through
a circle of blood was flexing the muscles
of a reptilian brain crazed and craving
to devour books, cities, innocence and people.
Our summer games turned into gore and thuggery.

           At the edge of the pond
          a nymph is stretched out
            waiting for the sun
            to crack its exoskeleton
          so that from its thorax
          a white-tailed dragonfly
          may emerge. Antlions dig
          circles in fine-grained soil,
         salivate their cocoon snare
           at the bottom of the pit
        and wait with their poison
           to paralyze their prey.
         A solitary bee clambers
        between pistil and stamen
         of a bittersweet, making
       its purpleblue petals tremble
        softly as the thin sibilance
       of mosquitoes drills holes
     into the morning for the past
to rush in like a horde of harpies.

Where were you
when they smashed babies
against tree trunks?

                    I was looking for my childhood

when they kicked Jews and Gypsies

                    I was playing hide-and-seek

trampled Marxists and homosexuals

I was going to be a fireman

till every bone snapped and dreams
ran with blood from mouths noses sex…

                    I was learning history
                    and sums:

                                      Multiply the number
                                      of blind people by
                                  the number of savages
                                and divide by the number
                              of innocents: how many
                            million corpses do you get?
                            The answer is exponential:
                something to the power of the power…

We were Winnitou and Old Shatterhand
when SS Scharführer Sommer
hung young *Untermenschen*
testicles in boiling water
before tightening the cramp
iron to crack the brain pan.

                          O Haupt voll Blut und Wunden…

                              Suffering has no season
                              and bears no fruit.

                                  Where were you?

                              I was discovering Bach

                      and wet dreams.

                            Where was I?

          I was memorizing verbs dates poems:
amo amas amat amamus...
1918...1933...1939...*Wer,
wenn ich schriee, hörte mich denn...?*

There were no angels winging goodwill no devils
  no omniscient gods watching SS Oberschar
    führer Moll line up women naked by
      a clay pit to target practice at
        the bull's eye in the dark
          triangle of hair he
            had all the
              angles
              cover
                ed
                wi
                th
                bl
                o
                o
                d

What if I had known
of cattle cars and gas chambers
had known to read
the voice of patriotic villainy?
Would I could I
have screamed loud enough
to shake an order of unreason?
Would I be here
to bear witness
to the pain
and the shame?

                    Lost in the scorched
                    and toppled streets
                    I was stumbling through
                    the ruins of my childhood
                    a kingdom laid waste
              by a lunatic piper from Braunau
                    who led a deluded people
                    to damnation. And I ran
                    through the burning streets
                    of my schooldays not knowing
                    where to turn to find shelter
                    not knowing what I was
                         that I was
                         looking for
                         home.

                                        Home? What home is there
                                           for the eternal wanderer
                                        but a long, dreamless sleep?

Home is here now
where memories can get lost
between summer and northern
lights, between the shrill
flight of geese and blackfly-
infested muskegs, between
lashes of snow and the warm
embrace of the Chinook. Here
you can always find a child-
hood or two by the shore
of a lake or on a prairie
farm a continent and a half
away from the scene
of your nightmares.

                         Go easy, heart,
                    on the sleep of prisoners.
                         The past is a cage
                         full of pain
                         and pitfalls.   .
                         At different times
                         different guards
                         have the same mugs,

                the same skulls
               in different places
              wear the same masks
                 we call faces.
               I recognize them
            in the censored newsreels
          from Cape Town and Chicago,
               Kigali and Kabul,
          Sarajevo Seoul and Santiago,
           Moscow Mogadishu Beijing
              Jakarta and Tel Aviv.

                        In their eyes I see the barbed wire
                          fences that have become camps
                       for refugees prisoners—men women
                       children their faces etched with fear
                     and hunger in the pandemic of tyranny
                    forced into exile from their own history.

O Tyre, mistress of the Mediterranean,
whose thin-spun silk once limned
the pleasures of Cleopatra, you
withstood Shalmanser and Nebuchadnezzar.
You're at the mercy now of those
who have no mercy: they found the pretext
they were seeking to rape you.

                Gun barrels roar against
                the innocent once more
                to exalt a general's ego,
               once more tanks thunder
               through the cash registers
                of arms manufacturers,
                 crushing the hands
            of peasants wresting a home
             from the recalcitrant land,
              and once more planes
           disembowel cities, tearing out
           streets, gutting homes, blast-
            ing whole families to hell
          to swell the bosoms of god's
           Chosen, the Swiss accounts
              of wheelers and dealers

                    relaxing before breakfast
                    in a warm bloodbath.

Tyre, Sidon, Damur, Beirut—
the peace of Galilee
is a web of lies. Black
smoke sears and surges
as once above Warsaw
and Cologne—a noxious cloud
telltale of an idiot race
burning all that is gentle and free
in the crematoriums
of messianic fantasies
and delusions of grandeur
leaving ashes, ashes everywhere.

                                        Does it matter
                                   when everything
                                     is burning
                                  to ashes, when
                        even matter itself is mortal?

                            Each proton decays
                            into an anti-electron
                            seeking to encounter
                            an electron jointly
                            to vanish without
                            a trace in a burst
                            of gamma rays.

              What place the heart
            where you and I add up
            to zero? What of the mind
          when all the possible worlds
        have run round two or three
          dozen zeros till there is
               nothing left other
              than the equation?

Lend me your ears, fearful captive
reader, I can smell you far back
to the primal soup, even under
the rain of ashes drifting through

this maple and spruce forest, even
with my senses mad. I want you
to listen to the sunlight stalking
shadows on moccasined feet
and to the grasses converting dung
into blossoms. Watch the bright
pink pouches of the lady's slipper
rise from acid bogs to lure the bumblebee
to push apart the veined lips and enter into
the ancient trade of nectar for pollen.
Insects make the world burst into flower:
the whole spectacle of colours
and the raptures of scent are but to entice
and seduce them—an arabesque of the senses
to embellish survival strategies,
a Bach fugue chasing its own flight
in the cave dwellings of the heart
where tears grow stalactites drop by drop.

    This is the month Franklin
     perished in the ice
    on his passage northwest
    where even the wind came
     black and ravenous
     to the frozen camp
    to lick their bones clean.
     It is the month Kafka
    died, begging his friend
     to burn the record
    of his nightmare journeys.
    They braved the void
     and found an end
     in their travels.

      Energy creates worlds from nothing
    in the emptiness which makes movement
    possible: space is an invitation to move
     to keep a rendezvous with time.
      Electrons flashing erratically
       at 600 m/s about their core
     make stone endure and timber hold,
     unleash the wind against mountains
    and cast whole continents into the sea,

                    temper the stars into distances
              and enforce a cold and eerie silence
                  upon a lunar night. They excite
                the cell to divide symmetrically,
             wrap the velvet flesh around their own
                   contrivances of blood and bone,
              and stir the mind to music and murder.

              In the molecular dance
                  of the universe
                  the hall too dances
                  and the floor spins
                      yet we are
                  the dancing-masters
                of our destiny we are
           what we do with what we are.

Put your ear to the ground
and check your pulse against
the earth's dark heart. Summer
is an invitation to lie naked
in the grass and let the green
fingers of the sun brush all
sorrow from your flesh. The wild
irises unfurl their blue
flags and ants climb through
hedge bindweed into the morning
glories trumpeting the golden
silence of approaching noon into thickets
where deep in the weeds a song
sparrow broods speckled eggs
on a moss-lined nest while its mate
chirps and trills as sprightly
as the light is long.

                         A flute, a badinerie,
                      a Bach suite—moment
                         of sheer joy dancing
                   through the open window
                       of an improbable world
                      where at any time jet
                   fighter planes thousands
                of miles away can scream

                      into your eyes and scare up
                      memories thousands of years
                      back in your own childhood:

    searchlights—bony fingers
      combing the night sky,
  skeletal hands plucking enemy
    planes from a black drone,
basements sandbagged, stifling
with the smell of urine and fear,
  air raid shelters, astringent
taste of damp grit, the short bark
 of anti-aircraft guns, the swift
downscale glissando of the bomb
that missed you, and after a heart-
stopping hesitation the fortissimo
  reaffirmation of your existence
  breaking every window cracking
 every wall for blocks, detonations
    with enough decibels to rupture
  your eardrums and decades later
    still devastate your cochlea.
The awesome silence that follows
is ashen, whimpering and sobbing
   with plaster in their hair
  mothers age in seconds, their
  children big-eyed, torn between
  terror and adventure, choking
   on cement dust and the in-
    comprehensible mad
     ness of this man-
     made apocalypse.

I've been there
and come back.
I've seen
the children
the bombs
didn't miss:

                a bundle of bandages wound
              immaculately like a fresh mummy
               with a single slot for the mouth
                  where the nurse slips in
                     the bottle to feed
                  the napalm-fried infant.

                              Or the nine-year-old, shredded
                                by a cluster bomb, both legs
                               and testicles blown off, looking
                                at night for his itching feet.

            Atura hal junna hissi?
            Are my senses mad?

The harpsichord is lost now
in the woodlands of Glengarry
the last chord skimming silver-footed
across a stagnant pond. A flicker
chiselling rapid-fire a dead elm
is gentler than the images
drilling into my heart's core.

                   A twelve-year-old, skull
                and spine broken under the rubble
                   of her home, her left ear black
                    and silent, her left eye blind
                with blood, her damaged brain dreaming
                       of life as a ballerina.

                                      Huda, Ahmad, Wafa—
                                    why is it my childhood
                                  memories have Arab names?

Sometimes there are pictures
from Lebanon that bear
names from my childhood:
Klaus, Inge, Lech, Kasis, Mordecai—

                   You cannot hear me
                    though I testify
                     on your behalf.

I heard the general declare: *Why
should we distinguish between
civilians and soldiers? No one can
teach us to be human.*

> Who said that?
> Heinrich, Jarek, Menachem?
> How to distinguish
> yesterday from today
> when no lessons are learnt?

> Suffering is not a function
> of names, but of faces.

Is this defenseless city
Warsaw or Berlin
Hiroshima or Beirut?
Bombed and shelled
into a lunar wasteland,
climax to a *Blitzkrieg*
against the unarmed,
last act of the *Götterdämmerung*
of some deluded *Herrenvolk*.

> *Joshua fought the battle of Jericho
> and the walls came tumbling down.*

> *Carthago delenda est.*

> *Wir werden ihre Städte ausradieren!*

Is this a true audit
of history, certified
by the chartered accountants
of our aspirations? I know
the generals ordering food
and water supplies cut off
are the same who own shares
in arms and munitions, but
their soldiers are the patients
in the hospitals they shell,
the teachers and students
in the schools they burn.

The same marionettes
pulled by the same strings
of money, slogans and pride
in this global village theatre
of profit and loss? Listen:

> *Of the cities of these people*
> *thou shalt save alive nothing*
> *that breathes: thou shalt*
> *utterly destroy them!*

Thus spake Yahweh
in a testament that is holy
only to creatures surrendering
any claim to the future.

> The cockroach can survive
> without mythologies
> levels of radiation
> that will exterminate us.

Are we to be
executioners
merely
of arithmetic
sentences
the cosmos passes
on all and sundry
predictably
at random?
Marionettes,
you and I,
in a nuclear theatre,
blocked by forces
weak and strong,
gravity and
electromagnetic waves,
destined for the scrapheap
of a preposterous history?
All of us victims
of our own mythologies?

Every child is a future
where a man or a woman
can be free and equal.
Chosen people make terror
reasonable and love
impossible.

>
> Confined to chance
> orbits halfway
> to the stars
> you and I are charged
> with self-perpetuating,
> like electrons circling
> hectically the dead
> centre of life, moving
> in the emptiness only
> an embrace can endure.

In the mountains of the Lebanon
where rivers once fierce have cut
deep valleys tortured to the sea
I hear six-year-old Bandali sing:
> *Give me back my laughter*
> *give me back my doll*
> *give me back my childhood*
> *give me back my home.*

Her childish voice echoes inside me
louder than the banging and bellowing of war.
It carries the burden of its elegy on the back
of pastured slopes, drifts down meandering
streams, lingers in olive orchards or over
the aromatic elegance of cypress trees,
a song looking for deliverance in sacred
groves where a gentler god once raised cedars
majestic from the ground to stand arms out-
stretched to bless the beauty of this land.

> Can a jet-fighter pilot
> on a supersonic reconnaissance
> mission hear the song or
> identify the cedars,
> smell the eucalyptus?

                                                    Our humanity is
                                                 an inverse function
                                                        of the speed
                                                   at which we pass
                                                        each other.

The train whistles and howls wild
and doleful across the apple trees,
like the howl of a wolf desperate
to be heard in another dimension.
It hurtles towards noon oblivious
of the colonies of wild blue phlox
bending to the pressure wave,
of the squirrels mating in the pine
and the tachinid fly that oviposits
behind the head of a caterpillar,
its larvae parasites destined to devour
their host. Once or twice more the train
howls shuttling drowsy travellers
between a handful of cities spared
the sound of bombs except in the sleep
of those who cannot forget and are still
learning to forgive

                  while across an ocean and a half the Hasbani
                       still carries the last stars downstream,
                  and grey-haired Mt. Hermon, *Jabal al-shaykh*,
                       looks eastward waiting for Castor and Pollux
                  to fetch dawn shivering from faraway deserts.
                       Westward in the direction of the sea
                            the night is bleeding into dark
                            valleys beneath a horizon on fire.

                    How can you tell
                    one burning image
                    from another through
                    the prism of your tears?
                    The Warsaw ghetto or
                    a Palestinian refugee camp?
                    Photos from a doomsday book:

/a group of women, an old man,
children, their arms raised
in surrender to the uniforms of
gun-toting terror, in their midst
a small girl stunned in her mother's
skirt, a muskrat paralyzed with fear
in a steel trap/

/teachers, scientists, artists
blindfolded, roped together like
camels, stumbling through ruins:
*all of a sudden they are
a bunch of nothings*
the victors' caption reads/

/a mother lifts
her dead child
blood-spattered
to high heaven
with a piercing
wail that should
move the stars/

Is this the way the world ends
—in Warsaw and Treblinka
in a blaze of firestorms and furnaces
incinerating all that is gentle and good
—in Sabra and Shatila
in the glare of magnesium flares
lighting up the night officially
for a massacre of innocents?

Atura hal junna hissi?
I hear the poet sing
Khalil's pain I hear
the shot ring out the shame
Khalil's pride I hear
the bullet sever the song
from the blood of Khalil
who would not sing
after the fall of the city
had driven his senses mad.

Where shall the birds fly
after the final sky?

                                          Onehundredandsixtythreethousand
                                                light years ago in the Large
                                                Magellanic Cloud a giant star
                                                collapsed under its own gravity
                                                until its iron core caught
                                                fire and blew apart, ejecting
                                                its elements into space
                                                with enough energy to incinerate
                                                any nearby solar system
                                                and seed new ones farther away.
                                                Among stars birth is
                                                like death a cataclysm
                                                without survivors. Only
                                                onehundredandsixtythreethousand
                                                light years away is a supernova
                                                a spectacle to delight the awed
                                                mind on the threshold of madness.

I lie in the moist grass trying
to banish the ghosts of yesteryear
from the dishevelled circle of clouds
where even a friendly face drifts
too lightly into a grimace. Down
here the grotesque air is green
and the earth's dampness cools
the troubled shades. A spittlebug nymph
is drinking alfalfa upside down
from a plant stalk, converting sap
into a froth cocoon. It has no receptors
for the rush of music skipping
with measured step between blades of grass
and round wildflower stems, impetuous
as some long-repressed need for joy
and affirmation, bursts of strings and brass
chasing each other through baroque tangles
of underbrush till they drop out of hearing
in the somber corridors of the bush.
Are the bees dancing to Bach
among the clover or is it only
my thoughts, my fancy—this summer
saraband in an alien land?

                              A swarm of redpolls puts some colour
                                  in the hemlock tree. I hoist myself
                              into the tall day, leaning on their chatter,
                              and scare up a groundhog. Stretched high
                                  on its hindlegs, it eyes me, rigid
                              as a taxidermist's pose, except it cannot
                                  stop munching. Fat and devious
                                  it devours the sprouts of peas,
                              beans, spinach, the whole gourd family
                              I planted. Rage explodes in the dark
                                  and convoluted spaces of my skull
                                  and hurls murder into my eyes...
                                  I take aim, my crooked index finger
                                      feels pulls the trigger—
                                          Is this the passion
                                          that turns Ariel
                                             into a butcher
                                       and makes a mockery
                                       of every Bach chorale?
                                          The alien intruder
                                          threatening our dreams,
                                          spoiling our circles?
                                  In days of fear gods bless night
                                  and bombs. In the territories
                              of fear an eye calls for an eye
                              and the clenched fist promises peace
                              when money is the measure of love.

But you cannot buy the stars
and if you sell a brother or sister
you have invested in a holocaust.
The world's battlefields are quagmires
of blood and guts that have sucked
heroes and cowards alike to their foul
deaths, the naive and the fanatic
perishing with their pain in the torture
chambers of history as nations, races
and religions take turns at being victims
and victimizers in orgies of slaughter
and sacrifice madmen organize
to maintain the privileges
of those who have not
earned them.

		Russians Germans Arabs
		and Jews, Christians
		Muslims Fascists—
		all labels tell you
		is the disease:
		xenophobic epilepsy
		ideological elephantiasis
		messianic carcinoma
		the master-race syndrome...

                                        Can the sun
                                        can anything
                                        save us
                                        cure us
                                        from ourselves?

June is the month that lights up
the north from horizon to horizon
stretching the days more than halfway
around the globe, growing galaxies
in the leaves of every tree, hatching
schools of sun in every ocean breaker,
placing a sun on the wing of every bird
and insect, the tip of every reed
and grass, in the belly of every drop
of rain and in the hearts of all
who flounder between fear and fulfillment.

            Skeletons under the skull
            dance in darkness and reach
            for light in the retina.
            I come away with
            only an eye full
            of images:
            the three-year-old
            with her throat cut,
            the castrated boy,
            women raped, piles
            of mutilated bodies,
            a bulldozer manoeuvering
            with shovel full of corpses
            starved till the parched skin
            could barely hold the knobbed

bones, harrowed till the mind
could no longer endure living
the pain the living pain of
dying the pain the stars
cannot know the pain...

                        This pain too, like all we know,
                 joins the procession of memories
                     that move peristaltically
                 in the pilgrimage of San Isidro
             Goya painted in the Quinta del Sordo
       across the scorched landscape of this age.
                   Enterrar y callar. I cannot
               bury them and be silent. I hear
              the voices, the endless march
                of prisoners and victims—
          victims of war, prisoners of lies,
         victims of conscience, prisoners
           of fear: they drag the chains
       of grief and guilt down the blood
   tracks across the sands of this century.

A carnival parade led by the king of fools
surrounded by blind musicians playing drums
and trumpets to pious time servers:
they award the peace prize to a terrorist
on a float of booby-traps and land mines.
Black uniforms goose-step faceless hoisting a banner
ONLY VIOLENCE CAN PUT AN END TO VIOLENCE
behind a blond strumpet carrying a pirate's flag
with a skull whooping in a shrill, mechanical voice:

              black is white
             might is right—
       pick your enemy and fight!
             Have your fill
            make your kill—
       war is money in the till!
             Better dead
          than pink or red—
     there's no more to be said!

Para eso habéis nacido.
Is that what we were born for?
A cradle made from barbed wire
and in it the torso of a girl singing:

>*give me back my laughter*
>*give me back my doll*
>*give me back my childhood*
>*give me back my home.*

> Tears wash the eyes
> but they blur the vision.
> They make old wounds
> burn without washing
> the past off your hands.
> You can build a house
> on the ruins of someone else's,
> but you can find no home there.

> Yesterday's Jew is
> today's Palestinian.

Every refugee camp cries out
bears witness against us—
in Pakistan, Sri Lanka, Vietnam,
Chile, Honduras and Uganda,
in Mozambique, Namibia, Sudan,
in Turkey, Korea, Lebanon—
we've driven millions
from their homes into
a world of camps where
children die of diarrhea
and the destitute receive
their dignity as handouts
in shantytowns. The dream
of universal brotherhood
lies shattered in tin can
shacks and cardboard tents.

> History is wasted on us
> if we inflict our own
> persecutions
> on others
> unless we bury
> vengeance in the barbaric caves
> of our heart.

> Beirut is burning.
> Palestine's people
> are on the move again
> looking for home.
> Where shall the birds fly
> after the final sky?

A dream is burning to the ground
and from the ashes rises the raven
of separation to pitch its caws
across the river where Tammuz' blood
flows still through the valleys of Hasbaya.
The raven flies black and shrill
through fig orchards and pomegranate groves,
its shrieks sharp knives to stab the hearts
of mourners weeping and wailing in red-
roofed villages for the dead who wanted
nothing but a home.

> Jerusalem, cradle
> of three faiths,
> and not one gesture
> of grace to trade
> in Beirut's kidnapping
> bazaars against
> an innocent victim
> or cut the barbed
> wire between the two
> cities where it's easier
> for mountains to meet
> than for an eye
> to encounter an eye
> without shame.

> Your shame is my shame
> and my shame is your shame.

Reflected ghostly in the window
my eyes stare me in the face,
burning with the shame of being
human. A feisty crow freefalls
from the top of the spruce tree,
a bold black slash across my mouth.
It banks against the cedar-shingled
roof with a scream alarming enough
to scare away the plaintiffs from
my childhood, and plunges headlong
into the bush vanishing between
wildly staggered soft-edged planes
of green and grey on wings wafting
calmly like large pine branches
awash with shade and silence.

        And there—across the frosted glass
of my mind I see a procession of men
and women carrying the star of David
trembling above them in a blue wind.
        Shame is written on their faces
and *Shame* they shout in the streets of Tel Aviv—
300,000 voices hurling their protest
at police cordons and Mossad cameras:
a chorus of the living
believing in a world to come
where to be is not to kill
but to love.

And suddenly the light is
as golden as the many yellows
into which van Gogh painted
his sitters, his flowers,
his fields. A flock of evening
grosbeaks flutters into maple trees,
their white tertiaries flashing
as they dance from branch to branch
agitated by a music I cannot hear.
Perhaps the spheres sing for them
to make a midsummer night's dream

come true. A rabbit sits erect
and scoops up a tall earful
of this hour's hums and whirs
whispers rustles and cracks
trills plashes sighs clicks
guggles smacks purls and swishes.

Who could've dreamt the bang that rent
a vacuum and smashed eternal darkness
into spacetime would ever cool down
to the temper of so faint and fragile
a music as orchestrates the balletomania
of life? Who could've dreamt the many
worlds compressed into a sphere of quarks
less than a billionth of an attosecond
old and no bigger than a Mackintosh apple,
a mere bite from which would've contained
all the galaxies and stars, all the nebulae,
gases, quasars and black holes, travelling
time immemorial at the speed of an explosion
away from a centre so small it would've fitted
in the palm of your hand? Who could've dreamt
the sun, the moon and our bluegreen planet
in that dense bubble of catastrophic patterns
of energy the potential for every possible
reality, including you and me, our struggles,
whether won, lost or ever engaged in, all that
we might have been and will never be, all
the journeys we might have taken plus the one
we do complete? And all that packed into
one hot big bang the size of a baseball
that threw billions of universes curved
across billions of light years to unravel space.

June is the month John Cabot
first caught sight of this old
continent aboard a ship no larger
than the human heart crammed
full of dreams and desires for a new
world in pursuit of the happiness
jewels, gold and spices could buy.
But God's pioneers came and planted
their delusions in native killing fields

            between bigotry and persecution, not
            knowing that light comes with lovers
               and creators, not with conquerors
                  who are the shadows cast by war.

Farewell, unquiet memories. I know
the thin wing of a mosquito outside
my window may fan the summer
air into a typhoon in the China sea.
This is the month a sick teenager
closed his eyes in fear and hatred
on a bridge in Sarajevo before pulling
the fanatic trigger: his shots killed
an archduke and his wife, sparking
a blood tide that smashed ancient houses,
swept empires off Europe's map
and twice set the world on fire,
its flames searing many a childhood.

                  I emerge from the chrysalis of memory
                     to reach out across half a century
                     to touch you, my unknown friend,
                  and your pain in the camps of death.
                  And I stretch my hands to reach across
                     an ocean and a sea to beat the *durbakki*
               drums alongside a young man in a refugee camp
                     in the mountains of the Levant. Together
                  we strike up the *dabka* dance, ancient circle
                  of lives more enduring than the walls
                     of cities or the cruel arts of invaders.

         Goldfinches flit through thorn bushes.
          Deep in the forest calypso orchids
         bloom magenta, their clusters of stamen
         tiny bursts of sunlight in the cool shade.
         A pair of sulphur butterflies spiral up
          and down about each other, rising higher
         and higher till they're dancing on tree tops
         and the male abruptly plumps down swift
             and bright as a meteor, followed by
               the fluttering caprice of the female,
         a lotus blossom floating down to her
           palpitating mate in the low creeping

                grass where a killdeer drags its unbroken
                    wing with cries of alarm theatrically
                away from its nest from its young from
                  its dupe till it is safe to break free.

Up north in the Truelove Lowlands
on Devon Island musk oxen shed their underfur
among the emerging bluegrass, foxtail and willow
herbs; they stand their desolate frozen ground
against men and wolves shoulder to shoulder
in a dark rosette—a primordial circle
that has kept ice ages and predators at bay.

5. When Africa calls Uhuru

> *Africa,*
> *Idle giant*
> *Basking in the sun,*
> *Sleeping, snoring,*
> *Twitching in dreams:*
> *Diseased with chronic illness,*
> *Choking with black ignorance,*
> *Chained to the rock of poverty,*
> *And yet laughing,*
> *Always laughing and dancing,*
> *The chains on his legs*
> *Jangling,*
> *Displaying his white teeth*
> *In bright pink gum,*
> *Loose white teeth*
> *That cannot bite,*
> *Joking, giggling, dancing...*
>   Okot p'Bitek, *Song of Ocol*

Nothing dissolves the mind's fogs as limpidly
as a summer morning mist forcing the outward eye
to look inward. Far away I see a black sun rise
that scorches deserts and steams up jungles
on a continent closer to my heart than all
the tall tales of religion. Once upon many
beginnings I was born there—so was this song,
and you, my uncertain reader. Once upon a crack
of ice or fire we put our feet on the ground
and walked, heads held high, the whole length
of Africa into this labyrinth of words echoing
uhuru from the Arab deserts in the north
all the way south to the cape of Zululand.

> *Uhuru uhuru uhuru*—
> is that the grey voice of an owl
> lost in the clouds that have come
> down to earth this morning?
> Dark call muffled in the damp
> gauze stuffed between ash maple
> pine and spruce that packs
> fields farms and fences,
> till nothing remains but vapour

and the world returns to some
primordial state—no shapes
no colour nothing but shades
of grey even the sun is no more
than a creamy smear
like some ointment
to heal an injury of nature.

                Out of the mist that hides summer
                from this dawn come voices
                once more voices worn thin
                travelling by chance between ice ages
                impact craters and continents adrift
                a Babel of voices spinning unrecorded
                histories from memories as webbed
                as spiders' nets, with meshes
                wide enough for whole generations
                to pass through, yet looped to catch
                what keeps the mind alive—voices
                their tongues lost to dust before
                they could tell the tale of a tribe
                that learnt to name a summer in the mist.

I hear the winds of history throb
in the jibs and mizzens, mainsails
and lateens of argosies, caravels,
dhows and galleons hugging a fickle
coast from cape to cape struggling
against a hostile sea I hear the plash
of oars the soft crunch of keels
in the sands of Abidjan DeKaap
and Zanzibar I hear commands
curses shouts and prayers in Arabic
Portuguese Dutch English French
as men come ashore to discover
a dark continent they never knew
deep down at their own hearts' core:
a black paradise where the adders
and vipers of their worst nightmares
had made their nests aeons ago.

The sun is devouring the morning
mist now and a familiar summer world

fades into focus image by image
like a photographic print in its developer
nameless silhouettes densing into leaves
branches—a tree! greening as grass ferns
shrubs vines flowers precipitate still nameless
from grey wisps like a green rubbing on tracing
paper a full spectrum of greens concocted
in the chlorophyll mills of every plant
an Ontario flora surfacing in waves
between 495 and 515 nm that make July here
greener than a sea of emeralds. Then a footpath
the toolshed a fencepost loom—intimations
of a different kind: you and I emerge from dawn.

                The white men who melted from the mists
                    of the sea never knew the black men
                    who peeled from the shadows of trees
                    were the brothers and sisters they left
            thousands of generations earlier in search
                of fresh fields and adventures. Blinded
                    by divine delusions and the black gold
                    of slavery they saw only savages
              born to serve their needs and appetites.
                  Jungles deserts even the rivers
              with their errant courses resisted them
                  but treaty by treaty and treachery
                  by treachery they spread like a slow
                  terminal disease and cankered Africa
                when they thought they conquered it.

        Something called *uhuru* across the continent
          till the rains picked it up in their seasons
          and beat it into the trees and the forests
          drummed *uhuru* up and down the great rift
          valley between smoking craters and implacable
          escarpments where humongous herds of wild
          beasts thundered across grassland and rivers
          long before *uhuru* meant freedom long before
          language found meaning in a meaningless world
          and there was speech to utter or sense to heed it—

Suddenly a flock of starlings
sensing perhaps an early fall
scatter a last fog patch
in the trees with their high
pitched alarums like the chatter
of agitated monkeys I hear
out of the green and steamy heat
hissing growling grunting
and howling, croaking squealing
and baying, snarling roaring
belching bellowing and braying
voices everywhere the voices
of feeding mating and dying
fill every crack and crevice
in the silences of Africa's
teeming forests and savannahs:
a cacophony of life cresting
in the skull with a big bang.

                Could all that have been
                prefigured all the myriad
                  forms of life struggling
                to adapt to the never
              ending upheavals of oceans
             and continents and that last
              blood-stained chapter
              from stone to stromatolite
            to stock-market—could all
            that have been contained
                in the unimaginable
              fraction of an attosecond
              before the atom before
        the quark even before Planck
time at the tredecillionth part (10^{-43})
                of a second of there being
                 anything at all and not
              rather nothing when the four
              forces that hold everything
              everywhere in place now
              were one and indivisible
                in a space tinier than
                a single proton that
                contained everything

          we know and can ever
          come to know? How
         do you get from nothing
         to the stars and trees
        and from there to misery?
       In that singular atto-moment
       of perfection outside space
        where was the flaw
        that put pen to paper
       to ask the question why
       put pain to pleasure
      in that singular and ultimate
      black hole where everything
       was nothing why four
         forces one and
          indivisible
          fractured time
          into galaxies
        why the sun why
        Africa why the
        question any
          question
          why you
           why
            I?

In the large picture window of my study the sun
now paints a summer landscape in silent motion:
clouds the mist raised trek eastward across a blue
savannah like a never-ending drive of shaggy
primordial mammoths in search of grass and water
shooed by the wide gestures of ash and tamarack
whose branches wave them on solemnly as in some
slow motion wind the tall tern spruce nods gravely
at the mystery it mediates between heaven and earth.
From the green scramble on the ground foul smelling
cow parsnip thrusts umbels at the light, the barbed
devil's club whose septic spines have pierced many
a moccasin and legging is ripening red berries
clustered like drops of fresh blood over large green
leaves. Treehopper nymphs tumble from elm twigs
to moult in the clovered grass into bugs that mimic
black thorns or green excrescences birds overlook.
A bluejay swoops down, its shadow screaming—

screaming at whom? Rosita's
eyes stare at me unforgotten
and unforgetting from the jungle
foliage looped in my skull.
Her spring has come and gone
but I see her pain still
in the eyes of children
everywhere. Though all
the saxophones in Dixieland
lament, the world goes on
spinning its idiot tales
of blood and tears over
and over: today it's Kigali,
yesterday it was Mogadishu
and Sarajevo, the day before:
Soweto Beirut El Salvador
East Timor the West Bank
Northern Ireland South Vietnam
on and on tomorrow and tomorrow…
In what Africa of the heart
was violence born? I've watched
the big cats in the wilds
of Kenya and found them fierce
in defence and feeding, but tender
with their own and tolerant
of others. What happened
on the way to wisdom?
Where? When? Why?

        Comets and asteroids struck time and again
      shaking our planet to its molten core shaping
a *terra infirma* in cataclysms of oceans and continents
   extremities of climate and atmosphere the violence
  of earthquakes floods cyclones volcanic convulsions
    Permian Norian Cretaceous in countless nameless
       catastrophes over and over yesterday's victor
      vanquished today till land and sea were left dead
  for millennia as trilobites lycaenops and dinosaurs
   along with countless species too bizarre for words
      vanished forever in evolution's teeming blind
        alleys where a shift of air or water current
      can make the fittest unfit for the new world.

Beginnings? Where
did *homo sapiens*
begin? Begin what?
To breathe? When we
crawled from the sea.
Why? To eat and be
eaten. Why? To live?
Why live? To talk?
To think? Yes think
why think why
when all I must do
is eat and make
love?—Love? Why
when did it begin?
In the stromatolite
four thousand million
years ago where one
celled bacteria learnt
to use light to make
sugar? Those same
immortal chloroplasts
toil still in every plant
to feed all living creatures.
Or did the human
tragicomedy begin
when the triassic curtain
rose and a reptilian
mouse appeared on stage
to manufacture milk
from sweat and learn
to climb trees and thus
survived two hundred
million years of predators
and cosmic violence
to become the first
primate?…Beginnings?

                                      July 1, 1858: Darwin
                                      and Wallace published
                                      papers that abolished
                                      beginnings. There are
                                        only junctures and
                                      something is gained

>   in every change of
>   direction something
>   is inevitably lost.
>   A twitch in grey slime,
>   a gyral quirk or a twist
>   of vertebrae or chords
>   in the throat precipitated
>   the neocortex that posits
>   probabilities fifteen
>   billion years earlier
>   to create a universe
>   *ex nihilo fit*
>   by a law too simple
>   for human understanding.
>   What has no beginning
>   for us must begin too.

Once upon a thousand times ice crusts co-opted
rains to creep miles thick south and north
from the poles, compacting rock, reshaping
landscapes beyond recognition and forcing life
to redesign scales as pelt and fur, and to retreat
into the shrinking territories of the sun.
In the unforgiving drama of dying and adapting
a hairy simian had gained a firm grasp
on branches reprogramming feet to move hand
over hand and relocating eyes to get perspective
on a green world and turn flat images
into solid objects that remained nameless yet
for another fifty million years. Now that drought
thinned forests squeezed in the tropic vise
deserted him australopithecus thumbed his nose
at ice ages and vanishing habitats and walked
straight into savannahs beyond all horizons
to test among sabre-tooth cats and elephants
the tools that make us killers and creators.

>   They came from Europe to all
>   the coasts of Africa in the garb
>   of culture, treating natives
>   like savages for they were savages
>   themselves—despite the chamberpots
>   replete with whiskey and wisdom

they came to empty in Africa and
refill with the continent's riches.
What they called trade was plunder
for they bartered at the point
of their guns, practising the art
of humiliation on a people who had
mastered the arts of bronze
and ivory, who knew how to carve
wood into ecstasies, how to cast
iron into tool and weapon, and
to fire terracotta long before
a Palestinian carpenter preached
universal brotherhood to those
who came to deny it, laying waste
the black man's courts and kingdoms,
ripping apart the fabric clans
and tribes had woven over the millennia
to contain pride and anger, scorning
their songs and dances that nurtured
the bonds of fellowship and affection
greed corrodes quick as an acid
iron. An unholy trinity of merchants
missionaries and military sat
at sundown, and mocked Africa,
casting lots as black men rounded up
their brothers and sisters
and sold them to be slaves.

In the harbour of Dakar
on Gorée Island stands
a slave house, its walls
saturated with the cries
of a hundred million
men women and children
whose only crime was
the colour of their skin.
Herded into pens they were
measured and examined
—the men's muscles
the women's breasts
the children's teeth—
and those found wanting
or sick were tossed out

the door right into
the sea as fodder
for sharks. The others
waited in darkness:
ankle irons spiked
through the foot and
itenu rings driven
through the lips
to quell the rebellious
they were fattened
to 140 lbs to fetch
the best price for
a voyage in the dark
holds of pestilent ships
where one third of them
perished, the rest
auctioned off across
the ocean to be
whipped and worked
chained and lynched
at white folks' pleasure
or displeasure.

    Africa, you still bear
    the stigma of our shame
    though those who left
    as slaves are free now
    because they did not
    shut their mouths
    and they would not
    forget their songs
    forget their dances:

    Blow man blow
    that horn man
    blow the blues
    tongue that reed
    slide the pitch
    smooth as skin
    the cymbals whisper
    shake it baby
    let the drums shake
    an' swing the flesh
    ain't no one there

*to take care
of you an' me—
jus' you an' me*

*paw that bass man
till the blood sings
blue the blues bro'
let the trumpet yell
at sun an' moon
life's a grief an' a thrill
baby move baby
wind down the day
pluck the strings
like they's nipples
ain't no one there
to take care
of you an' me—
jus' you an' me*

*jazz up your lovin'
the night is hot an' sweet
we ain't goin' nowheres
jus' dancin' to the beat
life's a kick an' a jump
lonely as the stars
in your eyes
baby oh baby
move it shake it
while I blow
my heart out
ain't no one there
to take care
of you an' me—
jus' you an' me.*

In the hush that follows I hear
the cries and groans of tortured
flesh. The drummer yes, the singer
the philosopher yes, but is it cool
to listen to a drunkard slaughter
his own kind, to a big mouth
commanding executions, a noisy
half-wit who dismembers his own wife,

or a savage who enjoys flogging
thieves to death with rifle butts?
Their victims' cries darken Africa's
skies: no other animal on earth exacts
such punishment from its own. Every
continent is awash with premeditated
self-inflicted human pain and misery.
Are homicidal maniacs the measure
of a species that struggled for five
million years up the brain's convoluted
paths to reach the light at the end
of the tunnel of its five senses?
Must consciousness either remain
dormant in the mists of unknowing
or wake up and walk Okot p'Bitek
hand in hand with Jean-Bédel Bokassa,
Louis Armstrong with Idi Amin,
Martin Luther King hand in hand
with Joseph Désiré Mobutu, and
the madman of Moroni with Nelson
Mandela—marching in syncopated time
uhuru beyond good and evil
where the way up is as the way down?

    Eyes take the measure of far flung valleys
where Africa is tearing itself apart inch by inch
and peer through a blue haze fed by volcanoes
the exhalations of life and the dust hoof herds
and wind-hoses raise—black white-edged eyes
glistening keen survey an obscure map of colours
shapes shades and movement for signs of food
and danger. The stars stirred no great longing
in the night though a tiny skew in the spine had
already launched their descendants on a flight
to the moon. Aeons passed speechless as mountains
rose and sea levels fell. Speciation flourished
while forests died giving a chance to the crafty
young grasses which had harnessed the wind to spread
a treeless savannah across whole continents—a vast
green carpet to welcome all the world's cats and cattle.
And they came: lion and leopard, aurochs and horse,
forcing *homo habilis* to spend a couple of million
years reengineering his hindlegs and perfecting the art
of walking before his elevation to the rank of *erectus*.

The sun is soaring toward noon.
Outside my study tufted vetch
coils tendrils through the grass.
Alfalfa butterflies tumble back
and forth between flowers up
and down like lemon petals
in an eccentric wind. Yet
the air is so still the buzz
of insects is loud enough
to mimic a distant plane.

                          I dream of Africa where fossils
                      speak louder than the follies
of superman. From the remote
aegyptopithecus whose passion
for fruit high in the trees
made them four-handed
to *homo sapiens sapiens*
whose larger brain has
yet to accommodate wisdom—
a handful of teeth must tell
the tale of a million generations
and trace the thin red lines
through the trials and errors
of primates as species and sub-species
come and go through the rapidly
revolving doors of evolution.
Wit and will like speed and strength
are at the mercy of pure chance.
If the Cretaceous comet had missed
this planet by a megameter
a sauronithoide might now
be writing this poem for a different
indifferent age of dinosaurs.
Or if the comet impacting Jupiter
today had crashed into earth
instead human history would end
tomorrow in a cloud of dust.
Would dinosaurs have made history
an idiot's tale like ours?
In the territories of the mind
nothing stands between the cannibal
Bokassa and Botticelli's Venus
but the sea and a different perspective.

Seeing is remembering. Because I was there
alongside you in a camp by the river winding
through the savannah, a small band we were,
moving with the seasons, our diet changed
from fruit-eating solipsism in the trees
to roots dug up and meat scavenged
that called for shared meals—we shared
everything: food, caves, children,
we shared the shade in the midday heat
and our bodies' warmth and needs at night,
we shared the stones to pound tubers
and crush bones to extract the marrow,
we slept on shared matted steads,
we shared grooming, gathering, guarding
and play—if we'd not shared you and I
would not be here to tell the story,
I know, I saw it with my own eyes
by the Mara river, saw what they saw:

    a herd of hippos cooling humongously
   in the muddy waters, their bulging eyes
  protruding from time to time like periscopes
    as they snort for air, flicking their tiny
  ears; on the embankment, immobile as logs,
  crocodiles, pinned down by the vicious light;
   behind them a troop of baboons, young
   and old, scampering through thorn bushes,
    noisy as a nursery, paying no attention
to the lion in the shade of a candelabrum tree
 courting his lioness as tenderly as any lover
  in heat, and when she is aroused they mate;
   just then three wart hogs appear, tusks
 curled like handlebar moustaches, they hurry
    single file across the clearing, stop
    curtly in their tracks, take in the scene
  and hurry on as though late for an appointment.

Where is the aggressor? Where aggression?
Not even the herd of elephants trumpeting
along the river can trouble the shared
territory: no imperatives to kill
except when hunger strikes or the young
must be defended. Sharing calls for

sounds and gestures of assent, not
for expenditures in violence and venom.

                              Beware of army uniforms
                              beribboned and bedecked
                          with medals like a buffoon's
                        costume: they are the primp
                    of butchers—like Idi the syphilitic
                who slaughtered three hundred
                  thousand of his own people
                      kept the choicest parts
                        of his choicest foes
                           in the fridge to eat
                  with an imbecile's bloodshot
                     eyes and slobbering grin
                  he crushed the pearl of Africa
               under his blood-spattered boots
                    till only dust was left
                      ashes grief and pain.

          Cry, my beloved Africa,
            cry for your women
            because the hyena
          of Uganda is not alone
      in his madness: too many
     men's manhood is nothing
      but spears and swagger.
          Your women carry
            your burdens
             on their heads
            and shoulders
            erect as bamboo
            they walk trails
          and paths through
           desert and jungle
      mountains and savannah
       they balance earthen
        water jugs and fruit
       from the fields where
        they seed and weed
        to wrest a harvest
       from stone and heat
         while their man

                    struts his cock
                    in the village
                    brandishing
                    his rhetoric
                    to prove
                    if all fails
                    at the point
                    of a machete
                    that he is
                    who he is not:
                    Simba the Lion!
                    and that he is not
                    who he is meant to be:
                    the man it took
                    threeandahalf
                    billion years
                    to wrest from the
                    intractable
                    elements
                    to come through
                    consciousness
                    to love.

Ask the women
whom age bends low
because they carried
too many bunches
of bananas too many
loads of bamboo and ebony
cane and cassava,
each of them
the fittest
vessel to carry
the seeds of love safely
through disease
and disaster across
a million millennia
beyond mutation and death—
ask them about pride.
Close to the ground
they move still
like slow freighters
heavy with the past's

consignment to the future
challenging you to join
hands in the dance of life:

Harambee!
the once saintly
Kenyatta called,
Let's all join together!
Paint your bodies,
paint your faces,
tie *lacucuku* rattles to your legs!
Beat the drums and
make a circle,
dance for rain, for seeds and harvest!
Shake and shuffle,
churn your belly,
dance for love, for death and weddings!
Stomp the earth and
sing to heaven,
dance for joy, for birth and sorrow—
harambee!

Laugh at the priest
fondling your full breasts
with his arid eyes
denying his lust and your dance.
Mock the soldier
with his gun
ready for the dance of war:
tell him to come
with a hoe to plant a garden.
Scorn the merchant
with his money
dancing on the bottom line:
teach him that the price
of life is love.
Shake your hips
and roll your belly
dance oh dance for friends and lovers
for today is
yesterday's tomorrow
a mango tree
ripe for picking

      when you dance and sing together
            make a circle
           for the spirits
            joy and love
        will dance forever
    in your hot and perishable flesh.
            Harambee!

       Croon man croon
        dark and husky
        as the jungle
        blood dances
        hot as head
       baby hold me
       feel me tight
      the bass baby
       the beat feel
    baby the drums
        call Africa
      cool man cool
    the music swings
    the piano shake
    you heart crazy
    shake she thigh
   and throw he leg
    blow man blow
     that clarinet
   high higher high
    baby blow me
      all the way
     to Africa blow
    me in the sky!

Today I'm back where my cradle stood:
it's as hot and humid, still and heavy here
as in the heart of any tropical rain forest.
A blue haze hangs in the listless trees
and even the sharp sumac looks limp.
The air is panting in a sweat, birds
are dozing under their feathers, frogs
gasp silently by the pond, the mosquitoes
have taken shelter in the cedars or
cling to the dank shadows under blades

of wilting grass. The day has developed
a breath smelling sweet and sour
of stagnant pools seminal ooze
and saprogenic slime. The deer-flies
are frenzied by the heat and attack
kamikaze style on delta wings, cicadas
wake up to shrill the torpor, and
the raspberries' red and pearly drupelets
look rich and lusty in the sweltering
light that suppurates from a glaucous sky
where the sun is fiercely coming to a head.

Our ancestors endured here
heat waves worse than this –
temperatures hot enough
to fry the brain, insects
larger and more lethal
than a poisoned arrowhead,
predators as callous
as the stone they fashioned
into tools, and parasitic
worms eating them alive
in stages of such pain
to put any inquisitor to shame:

                    the invisible armies
                    of amoebae bacilli
                    cocci spirilla and
                    viruses commanded by
                    the tyrannical sun
                    conquer the mightiest
                    conqueror; they give you
                    no choice: lockjaw
                    bilharzia leprosy
                    and hepatitis—dysentery
                    alone kills ten million
                    children under five
                    each year in Africa
                    where the ubiquitous
                    mosquito bites at random
                    spreading malaria
                    and yellow fever,
                    the tsetse fly

frantically injects
the sleeping sickness
whose coma is terminal,
the tiny buffalo gnat
lays its eggs
in any open wound
where they hatch
and ulcerate the skin
till river blindness
breaks out and kills you
unless the excruciating
itch from head to toe
drives you to kill
yourself first;
the filovirus will
blister your skin
rip your flesh
in shreds till you
vomit and cough up
your throat, your tongue
and your trachea
in bits and pieces
with black blood
and you succumb
to seizures
while parasitic worms
burrow through
their victims' insides
till they bleed
from mouth and rectum
with the green monkey
disease or hemorrhage
to death internally
with snail's fever
which still infects
200 million people
annually throughout
the disadvantaged world
—so many painful ways
to die, so few to survive!

Yet we date our succession
back billions of generations

directly to the primal ooze,
each one of us travelled
that desperate ecstatic path
to consciousness and even
our first bacterial ancestors
learnt that those who share
fare better in the battle
to survive. There never was
a paradise at the beginning:
it is an island dreams created
in a treacherous capricious sea.
There is only the horror and
the happiness of knowing being.

The ocean that gave birth to life
was not Homer's wine dark sea
or Botticelli's benign water,
nor even Shakespeare's wind-obeying
or Delacroix's tempestuous deep –
more soup than sea it was leeched
from molten rock mineral and ore
in a million years of rain between
volcanoes spewing perpetual magma
and asteroids the size of continents
comets meteors pummelling the planet
till all the elements danced
up a storm of atoms breaking
molecules down reuniting particles
by electrical charges and discharges
in a furious slop crater by crater
where amino acids time and again
joined forces only to be wrenched
apart again and rejoined
till a short single-strand RNA
catalyzed protein and by a random
felicitous mistake replicated
as DNA…and life began—
by the grace of amphiphiles,
hydrothermal vents, fool's gold,
or a gift from other stars?
Beginnings? Minerals know how to
replicate a pattern but they cannot
multiply. The first membrane formed

somewhere between amino acids
and nucleotides became the binding
for the book of life the DNA began
to write in a four-letter alphabet
etching a code in carbon blocks
that describes and determines all
that lives all that lived and all
that will ever come to live
by mitosis or meiosis chromosome
crossover inversion or point
mutation in the genetic spiral
whose elegant symmetry belies the crude
and blundering deviance of evolution.

The stone is but a step
from the flower and the worm
but a remove from the root
of trees. What separates
the mammal from the microbe
is only a matter of time.
We are the issue of exploding
stars that seeded a galactic
cloud and precipitated earth,
progeny of the rocks, cousins
to every plant and animal
under the sun. What their host
calls a disease is a feast
for parasites and death
is a hotbed for bacteria
and scavengers. Our world
has no seams: greening breathing
dancing and growing, feeding
mating dying and flowing
are the hop and the scotch
of nature's hazardous game
connecting all and everything
so long as the rules are not broken.

Who has the power makes
and breaks the rules
till the power breaks
him: Cpt. Jean-Bédel
needed a special

uniform for all the
medals he gave himself
till on a sizzling day
he made himself
*Sa Majesté impériale
l'empereur Bokassa premier*
in Bokassa Stadium on
Bokassa Avenue in
a coronation robe studded
with two million pearls
placing a $2 million crown
with a 138 carat diamond
on his head in a country
in central Africa with
an annual per capita
income of $250 and
250 km of paved highway
connecting the 250 imperial
statues and palaces—
his friend Valéry Giscard
footed the bills in the name
of another delusion of
power which stipulates that
a colony must remain
a colony forever if under
a different name a different
ruler the rules remain
the same: the poor grow
poorer because the rich
grow richer so long as
someone else pays
and Giscard (in return
for gifts of diamonds) paid
out of his people's pockets
for Jean-Bédel's madness
mayhem and murder
till the Imperial cannibal
clubbed 80 children
to death for refusing to wear
the new national school
uniform adorned with his
Imperial mug and medals.
'*He's not that bad,*'

    the wife of an American
    missionary told reporters
    with Christian charity,
    'there's complete religious
    freedom here.' After all,
   Sa majesté impériale converted
   twice back and forth between
    god's learned son and
    his illiterate prophet,
    depending on who paid
    how much, and he atoned
     for his slaughter
    by fathering 30 children
    on 9 wives—admittedly
    a far cry from the Master
    of the Spear who claimed
    to have begotten 500 progeny
     on 100 wives—still,
    the bottom line leaves
     only a net loss of
     50 children slain,
    which is *not that bad.*

Cry for your children,
my beloved Africa,
where my cradle stood,
for they are still
being murdered
or they die from hunger,
disease and heartbreak,
die before they can walk,
die before they can talk,
because their fathers
will not deny the rich
are growing richer
perfecting the cruelties
their colonial masters
invented, but bossman
is bossman black or white
the poor are growing poorer
hair curly or straight
and Africa is free now
to be its own master

and must master itself
to dance for its 500 gods.

                    Beware
               of the tidings
             of missionaries:
            they say *mercy*
          when they mean
               mercenary
            and *save*
          when they mean
                slave!
           They bring you
            to your knees
        with your eyes shut
         they rob you blind
          taking your land
      in exchange for some
     holy Humpty Dumpty
        from the nursery
      of Neanderthal man.

                                  The negro is a child,
                               said the once saintly
                               man from Lambaréné,
                        and children must be
                        chastised. Then he played
                              Bach on his organ
                     and attended to their pain.

Cry for your men, Africa,
because they deny their children
their humanity, deny them the dignity
of schools where they could learn
to turn words into wings to rise above
the slimy exchanges of money
and copulation, to fly to a cape
of good hope where they can be
free and equal under the black-hot sun.
Your men dream Mercedes Benz
instead of freedom though all
the valleys and their mountains
lakes and rivers from sea to sea
the plains and forests cry *uhuru*…

which means freedom is the path life has chosen
from prokaryotes to protozoa elaborating cilia
and flagella in the prison of their cells evolving
ever changing associations for three thousand
million years to constitute the first fish captive
of the sea struggling to turn fins into crutches
turning fins into legs for amphibians turning
swim bladders into lungs to live in the air
and run as reptiles the whole length of the land
to mammals climbing trees learning to walk
upright as hominids to propel themselves
beyond the wildest dream of any bird to soar
into space and escape the hold the earth has
over us and fly free *per aspera ad astra*.

    The path the primate took had many junctions
and more pitfalls than a terminal moraine.
From dryopithecus to this day we clambered
through a landscape in permanent revolt.
Gondwanaland is still exploding in slow motion
raising range upon range of heaven storming
mountains from the Alps to the Himalayas.
Heat waves are short interglacial recesses
when glaciers melting and with torrential rains
drill rivers through rock—Rhine, Danube,
Ganges, Volga, Mackenzie, and in Africa
they carved the sweeping course of Congo
and Zambezi, Nile and Niger, and cascaded
the waters of the Limpopo, Ogowe and
Volta fuming into the sea. But the ice
always returned, spreading from the poles,
sucking up the oceans to bury most of the land
under a lid of ice a mile thick until
the Mediterranean dried up and the estuaries
of the Nile and the Rhône became waterfalls
a mile down into the salt-crusted basin.

The ebb and flow of weathers and tectonics
left Africa in the shape of a heart
and placed it at the centre of the globe
midway between Asia and America, Arctic
and Antarctica, at the centre of life. Here
an ape met the challenge of an alien

environment and blood began to beat
in temples booming hot like a dark drum
calling all the world to consciousness.
Generations of primates came and went
driven by cold and curiosity scavenging
then hunting their way across the planet
fighting mock battles to maintain order
and returning taller bolder more skilful
always on the move tools chipped and flaked
always changing—the teeth the jaw the brow
more graceful, nomads following the migrations
of rivers and cattle grass and sunshine
turning grunts and squeals into bonds
of affection refining the clan and the vocal
chords growing more determined the hand
the walk the chin the skull more domed
till the brain had tripled and—there!

> they stood—the first *homo sapiens* couple
> coming to know their image in the still pool
> as their own knowing growing to love
> what they knew that they must be
> wanderers on a journey free to choose
> a destination in search of no matter
> where or why the true measure of the mind
> is a question mark. Perhaps they were
> moved to tears by what they felt they saw
> they knew in that shared unrecorded moment
> when millions of neurons fired and burnt
> an immemorial film from their eyes—
> in that first blaze they must have marvelled
> mute at the splendour and the mystery
> of the land- and lifescape stretched out
> below the mind's peak and they saw
> in a drenching rain the tears in all
> things as they listened to the dark
> thunder mourn a loss of innocence
> for which there are still no words.

Naming the world is like bringing
the lights up on stage. Things appear
to be where and what they are.
Each word recreates the world

giving it colour shape motion
place... and soon tropical birds
performed their ritual for the just
awakening mind in a paradise
of the imagination: the black and white
boubou with their bell-whistle-and-croak
routine deep in dark thickets;
the choral toogel-de-doogle
of the speckled red and yellow
barbet breeding among termites;
the shrill kingfisher diving
for small-fry on malachite wings;
the hornbill with casqued and curved
beak grunting like a lion as he
walls in his mate in a mud-and-dung
cell to breed; the lilac-breasted
roller in feathered finery
of a splendour fit for a wedding;
the long-legged secretary bird
stalking the savannah in silence;
crested with a headdress
worthy of a Bantu chieftain,
or any of the thousand birds
of Africa—the golden weavers
gregarious in their globed nests,
the parasitic whydahs, the multi-coloured
sunbirds glittering in flowering
trees, the spectacular bush
shrikes and parrots, bishops
cutthroats lovebirds and bee-eaters
waxwings turacos woodpeckers
white-eyes and pittas, the parasitic
flycatcher with its long cinnamon
tail and the red-faced apalises
singing in the desert scrub—
a chirping warbling cheeping
twittering piping trilling
squawking hooting and whistling
musical riot that left the first
man and woman speechless—

but they soon found words, words and
more words for to name is to share
and they came to know what the birds
in the air knew already and all the beasts
in the water and on land—that to share
is to survive and sharing they tested
and honed words and more words
for to name precisely is to understand
and they came to know what the birds
in the air and all the beasts in the water
and on land never knew—
that to understand is to be human.

    Thus *homo sapiens sapiens* was born in the great rift
valley when once again the advancing ice encircled
Africa and Tuba exploded with the force of a hundred
Krakatoas and blew 2,000 km^3 out of the earth into the sky
to beget a global winter of many years that only the fittest
survived. Where a geological day earlier, hippos browsed
in the blazing sun by the Thames, polar bears were now
hunting seals while to the south a most adaptable primate
rewired its brain and grew Broca's bump on its cranium
to accommodate speech and comprehension. Soon this
curious creature sharpened its tongue along with its tools
and outgrew the scavenging competition of vultures
and hyenas. As summer returned small bands followed
the receding ice, the men hunting wild oxen, red deer
and horses, elephants and rhinos, the women gathering
nuts fruit roots, the children laughing and learning—
they spread across every continent to begin their journey
to the stars, building spaceships out of words determined
to leave the birds to their trees and inhabit the skies.

    A languaged beast
languishes no more.
Words are oil
in curiosity's flames,
salt in the wounds
of ignorance and folly,
water on the mills
of invention—words
are the arsenic of anger
and the spice of love,

                    a poet's dream and
                a politician's nightmare,
                  for they name to tell
                   the truth; they make
                     all things appear
                  to be what they are:
                        debatable—
                   and in the heat
                of argument they are
               lost unless you raise
                 your voice to song.

I have travelled the seven seas
and every continent to sing to you
of my voyage that started before
it began and that will go on after
it ends. The whirlwinds of change
blow forever on these smooth coasts
pushing Africa across the equator.
I sing of the adventure of being
human. You and I are never
the same twice. Even as I sing
and you listen we move beyond
the words that express us.
We too have reached the equator
of our destiny. Our tools
and weapons have outstripped and
outmanoeuvered us on a power trip
that leaves our fellow-travellers
gasping. Even our knowledge
has left us to the mercies
of machines. I want to sing
but the cacophonies of hatred
are louder and I must bear
witness today for tomorrow
will soon be our yesterday.

                    Once upon a time war was a ritual,
                       the loser yielding place and mate
                      but not his life, a ritual enacted
                   by birds and beetles, whales, lions
                         and chimpanzees. Should not
                 the primate with the double wisdom

                    have been as smart? Instead
                Shaka with the tiny penis forged
                assegai into swords and slaughtered
                    his astonished foes. Forcing young
                and old, men and women, to bear arms
                    he marched killing and conquering
                        along the Umfozoli River to forge
                            a Zulu kingdom for his mother
                        Nandi, the Female Elephant. Bloody
                was his revenge for his diminished manhood:
                    witch doctors with dry gourds
                in their hair smelled out his enemies
                and with the black tails of wildebeest
                    condemned them to the fire-hardened
                    needle-pointed bamboo hammered home
                    with painstaking accuracy and slowness.

Apart from us, is there or has there
ever been among the vigintillions
of animals and species on this planet
past and present a single one capable
of forcing a needled-pointed stake
through the rectum up the spine
of a fellow-creature and enjoy watching
it writhe to death like a worm on a hook,
but with spine-chilling screams?

                When his mother the Female Elephant
                    died of old age Shaka butchered
                        scores of pregnant women
                    with his own hands to search
                    their entrails for the secret of life
                        and found only blood and gore.
                    In the dark days that followed
                    his nation foundered in a bloodbath
                    until he died like Caesar at the hands
                        of two brothers and a friend.
                    Mad Mzilikazi of the Matabele
                        rivalled Shaka's massacres razing
                    kraals crops and cattle. Between them
                        they created a *mfecane* that killed
                    a million people and left the survivors
                    in a wasteland of their own making.

What malice in nature permits
such monsters to be born and live?
The savages of Africa are no nobler
than the savages of Europe. Black
is a pigment of the skin, not a moral
or mental condition; it is the business
of dermatologists, not politicians. The art
of massacring the innocent was not invented
on the continent that gave birth to us.
Long before Ashanti warriors subjugated
their neighbours brutally to the Golden Stool
to found a kingdom, the armies of Greece
and Persia, Rome and Babylon, of the Huns
and the Vandals taught the world all there is
to know about pillage rape and slaughter and
at the Cape of Good Hope it was Kitchener
the Lord who invented the concentration camp
Comrade Stalin, Herr Hitler, and Chairman Mao
perfected along with Bosnia's ethnic cleansers.
For every Rwanda there are two Irelands,
for every Bangui three Buchenwalds,
for every Hottentot a score of Huguenots—
from Attila the Hun to Anton Pavelic, the butcher
of Zagreb, from the first city in Mesopotamia
to Mogadishu, from the Crusades to the Khmer Rouge
human history is a grisly calendar of atrocities.

>   Pink skin too
>   is a matter
>   of pigmentation.
>   Cruelty, thy name
>   is Man—
>   civilized Man!
>   Our most noble
>   dreams drown
>   in blood and tears.

>   I have watched vultures
>   rip wildebeest to shreds
>   and hyenas root in entrails
>   of gazelles with blood-
>   smeared snout, but they
>   were feeding on carcasses

                              not wallowing in the pain
                              of living kin—like the crack
                              Canadian paratrooper who
                              took 4 hours to beat
                              and kick to death Sidane
                              a 16-year old black
                              in handcuffs in a sand-
                              bagged cell 7 feet
                              by 9 feet to teach him
                              fear while his buddy took
                              snapshots with a flash
                              and his superiors listened
                              to the screams of the dying
                              boy one night in Somalia.

           If I were still as black
       as I was born long long ago
       I would not want to emulate
       a people who live by the cold
       knife of logic and remember
           only victories, who invented
             apartheid to give cruelty
             the face of reason. A giraffe
             cannot become a monkey,
             nor should a monkey want
       to be an Arab or an African.
       Let's search our own hearts
           and histories for the warm
       hand of compassion to show us
       the true road to freedom where
             defeat renders us human
       and human is understanding
       that we share and share alike
             the vulnerable flesh and
             the knowledge of our dying
             with all men and women
             and there must be a way
             forward that leads back
       to what the birds in the air
       and all the beasts on land and
       in the sea have never forgotten:
                 that we are children
                 of hatching and caring

                nestling nursing sharing
                    and sharing alike.

Even the books are sweating on the shelves
as noon approaches and I wonder if their authors
would approve my celebrating summer in sorrow.
Ideas too are mortal, their half-life measured
not in histories of wealth or war but by the light
they shed in the mind. The tall sunflowers
are gazing bright-eyed across the garden.
Would they if they could approve the war
between the wilderness and civilization
whose beneficiaries they are? The advance
of weeds and seedlings is relentless: wild
raspberry bushes with their clustered flesh,
bristling nettles and blazing-stars, juicy
milkweed with their hooded blooms, goldenrod
and devil's paintbrush, lilac-banded teasel
with their stout spikes, black-eyed Susan,
thistles, mustards, vetches, brambles
and ivies—all pressing whatever advantage
they have gained, using all the strategies
of shading thrusting crowding pushing
jostling to procure their place in the sun.
And we must confront them, keep them at bay,
eradicate them to secure the space we need
for ourselves and all the fruit and vegetables
we have bred too feeble to survive without us
the unforgiving free-for-all of evolution.
Is this the root of evil that we took sides
with the garden against the wilderness,
mastering nature which will be no one's slave?

                For millions of years
                our primate ancestors
                moved with the sun
                and rains, with the herds
                and grasses, learning
                to walk this planet
                crisscross, carrying
                only spear and stone,
                fire and the day's
                quarry and pickings.

        Night was home
        by a lake or river
        under a mutable
     moon and the stars
       floating radiant
and mute on the water's
  mirror where the first
     awed reflection
glimmered then ignited
and flashed in the brain
   the whole cosmos
thundered across the face
   of the earth the first
question as unanswerable
   as the last breath
  that made us nomads
of the seasons and the sky.

The fateful breakthrough came some fifty millennia ago.
By that time we were carving boats out of tree trunks
    to test the waters and shortly we reached Australia.
We'd eliminated most hominid rivals and soon assimilated
    the last of those burly Neanderthals: their big brains
were no match for our brawn. But we learnt a few things
   from them about herbal medicine and burying people.
We endured a few more chilling cold spells that lasted
   a couple of thousand years and induced us to tailor
  our own clothes, but the weather was getting warmer.
Things were improving all around. So we began to craft
    bracelets and necklaces, shape pottery figurines,
  ·   even paint pictures on the walls of our caves—
we were starting to appreciate beauty, and soon realized
we could do better than mother nature, that heartless bitch.
   Art was born. A regular barter trade in ivory, bronze,
   and ceramic adornments followed; we shared the profits.
The moon taught us how to divide the cycles of the sun:
  calendars are good for religion, keeping appointments
with the gods, and that's good for business because you feast
    better when you trade well. Hunting was good too,
plenty of animals, though we may have overdone it a bit:
    some of the large ones like giant elk, mammoth,
   woolly rhino and diprotodon disappeared—hunted
  to extinction they say. But there were more and more

of us, humans were multiplying around the world,
and we *had* to eat. That's when we made the discovery
that changed everything: we learnt to grow and raise
our own food: millet in Africa, maize in America,
rice in Asia, and sheep goats gazelles and oxen
everywhere. No more waiting for mongongo nuts
from fickle nature, no more running after antelopes
till your feet splayed like lily-pads. We made ourselves
independent and settled down to civilization, built
huts temples palaces and filled them with beds benches
tables even vases—and it was all ours: we made it
we owned it and we invented words and numbers
to keep track of things. No more monkey business
for us: for all their chattering and squealing when alarmed
they could barely tell a leopard from a python. No,
we found out what words were good for and we talked
and talked and we're still talking because talking
means progress and progress is what it's all about.

The neolithic revolution overthrew an order
of nature as cataclysmically as any comet.
It began perhaps in the valley of the Nile
whose waters the dark heart of Africa pumps
to the moon's rhythms to flood its banks
and prepare a fertile ground for growing
grain and raising cattle. Nomads settled down
to farming as home ceased to be a harmony
of shifting rains and the resilient ways
of beast and plant, and became a place to stay.
Campsites turned into hamlets, hamlets into
villages into towns and soon Jericho built
walls to protect its harvest from thieves
and *la dolce vita* spread to the valleys
of the Jordan, the Tigris and the Euphrates
till in Anatolia they were weaving cloth
in the first city, Çatal Hüyük, a streetless
hive whose five thousand inhabitants entered
their homes through the roof and buried
the dead under their beds after the birds
had picked them clean—urban civilization
was launched!
    Herdsmen who sat in the fierce
heat to etch into clay tablets pledges of goats

for the gods unwittingly invented money
and writing. To the north children of a lesser sun
changed colour to permit ultraviolet light
to pass through pink skin to produce
what the long winters deprived them of—
vitamins essential to the strength of bones,
while their parents tamed the first horses
whose descendants would carry apocalyptic hordes
from one end of the world to the other.
The harvest they reaped we call history.

        The seeds of war and malice were born
          when we began to work the earth
           for comforts and pleasures only
            power and wealth could buy.
        The larger your house the larger
        your appetite for things to put in it
        until you become so ravenous to own
        that you'll kill to slake your hunger, and
        by then you've built a still larger house
          creating a still larger appetite...

                Everything was implicit in the beginning
                which was no beginning if the universe
                is a closed system where probability
                puts things in their places though you
                can't be sure where anything ever is
                except on its way down for energy
                is constant and nothing is lost
                except form by the second law
                of thermodynamics life is motion
                is heat is irreversible even when
                the temperature was ten quadrillion
                degrees and light had only travelled
                three centimetres from nowhere a hundred
                picoseconds after nothing ceased to exist
                permanence had vanished from a vacuum
                to make room for entropy moving quarks
                to particles it was all settled a millisecond
                after reality became probable transience formed
                plasma atoms molecules elements life a whole
                universe composed of 18 quarks, and every creature
                wanting immortality makes dying copies of itself

            so that its kind will last forever—so shall we
            go on pursuing power when we know the copies
                aren't exact and the mistakes in time
              will turn our kind into another, leaving
              only a sketchy record of the dead ends
              in the DNA? Shall we go on killing one another
            when we know something is lost in every change
            in every transformation energy always runs down
              volts itself into other orders below the horizon
              of recovery so that the universe is cooling off
                and fifty sun years from now our star
                will grow hot and bloated with exhaustion
              and explode all myths of eternity spinning
                a ball of ash beyond any orbit of life –
              how can we not share the planet we share
            when we know we must share its fate?

They shared out Africa amongst fifteen European nations
wheeling and dealing in Berlin in 1884, like frenzied vultures
they tore a living continent to shreds, hacking and pecking
for the lion's share. High as euphorbia they sent their soldiers
to draw a map of Africa in their own superior image –
the arrogant English, the intolerant French, the brutal
Portuguese, the imperious Germans and the rest of them,
obsessed with overseas possessions they sliced and slashed
across 850 languages to stake out their claims in Akan
Bobangi Chewa Dagomba Edo Fulani Gandi Herero Kikuyu
Kiswahili Luo Xhosa Yao Zulu to cut across the lands
the territories of a thousand tribes and clans, Bushmen
and Bantu, Hamites, Kaffirs and Pygmies—and the
missionaries came with their pious anaesthetics the better
to rob Africa of its gods its legends its dances its gold,
and teach the natives the gospel of forgiveness and of scorning
worldly goods so that the merchants could come smug
with their air of euphorbia to relieve them of those goods
that were so bad for their souls, turning the richest
continent on earth into a poorhouse within a single century.

            It's always you and I, black
              or white, who must pay
           for the privileges of the pious
            and the powerful. The Che
          Guevaras and Bikos who would

          set us free become their victims.
        This is the month Jaurès, the people's
           warrior for peace, was murdered
           in Paris and the echo of the shots
         a feeble-minded Serb student fired
            reverberated in the corridors
             of profit and politics, sending
          Europe's statesmen into a shuttle
      frenzy to replace *la realité du monde*
        sensible with the illusions of war
         and victory in which Africa was
        but a pawn and for some a prize.

The ides of July have come
and the rainy season approaches.
Africa is calling *uhuru* across
its deserts, mountains and lakes
and the echo wakes the spirits
of the ancestors to dance with them
from the darkness of fear and superstition
into the light of freedom: *uhuru*
is the voice of its forests, rivers
and savannahs where a pageant of furs
and feathers, hoofs and horns,
stripes and spots celebrates
the improbable odds of survival.
Across the Serengeti plain
north through the Masai Mara
proud nomads still herd
their cattle with the seasons
where a lion pride rests and plays
under the umbrella of an acacia tree
side by side with a sly hyena
and a cheeky family of baboons
zebras graze amongst skittish
gazelles and wildebeest to hide
their giveaway camouflage; red-faced
the ground hornbill walk among them
muttering through their crimson wattles
while on a kopje where a lethal
puffadder sleeps a topi stands
tall as if to impale the sky
with its ridged horns, watching

the swift and abrupt impala
leap high and wide of nothing
anyone can see while above them
an eagle's cry draws ominous
circles no larger than a kraal
that narrow like a closing net.
In the big bush to the west
black mambas drape like lianas
over jungle branches and siafu
killer ants advance in deadly
formations that stop short of
nothing. Ants have crawled
and snakes slid and tongued
their devious ways voiceless
through a paradise of thickets
for two hundred million years
while apes and monkeys are barely
in their salad days, the bright-eyed
chimps agile in the canopy
and the gorillas lumbering already
into the last remote range
of their lives. By the watering-hole
at the edge of night the leopard's
throaty call troubles the thirst
of those who come to drink.
Darkness too feeds on freedom.
When Africa calls *uhuru* the echo
reverberates around the earth
for it speaks with the voice
of the birds in the air and all
the beasts on land and in the water
who have always known that life
is a celebration of just being there.

>
> This is the month
> Kafka was born and
> Jean-Jacques died.
> *Grimpez aux arbres,*
> *espèces de singes!*
> *Retour à la nature!*
> Journey from grey
> penthouse back to
> green canopy by

memories that were
even then infested
with snakes. Proust
was born this month
to search and find
his jungle Eden in
a cork-lined room
where he smelled
his way back
to many beginnings.
Something was lost
on the way to the city
for Joseph K. to wake
and discover freedom
was his prison
or else why
would any human
turn into a beetle?

Houses are the atoms that constitute cities
temples and palaces the atoms of power
combine easily to form the molecules of hatred
and war unless you block the reactions
of greed and fear that catalyze them. Houses cry
for windows and windows cry for air and light.
Beware of those in pursuit of power, whatever
colour their skin, however pious their mask,
lest they put shutters and bars on your windows
and lock your doors, for power needs victims
and henchmen to violate you throw you
scraps so you'll violate others to get more
scraps for power is voracious as vultures
and money is power's club, it will put you
in your place buy your women, your sons
your daughters, and sooner or later your mind
and your heart, turning temples and palaces
into prisons till it possesses everything,
consumes everything till all that is left
is to consume itself
leaving a wasteland—
like Rwanda

where in a single month
half a million children
women and men were clubbed
hacked stabbed chopped
kicked and gouged to death
by their good friends and
neighbours disembowelled
decapitated and left to rot
in their kitchens and bedrooms
in the fields and by the roadsides
till a stench more putrid than
the one-day bloom of a thousand
stinking euphorbia flowers
drove the people from their homes
their families their villages
to escape genocide the Tutsis
and the Hutus like the Ibo
slaughtered till the rivers
ran black with blood shed
by black clubs and machete
the survivors fleeing between
Jalaf and Khalif, too famished
to run for their lives
through Angola and Mozambique,
Somalia and the Sudan,
Namibia and Zaire, men
dragging their indignities
through the dust, women
balancing their poverty
on their heads, and harried
children, with names as
auspicious as Lakayana
and Mamadow, but with eyes
like Rosita's full of the pain
and horror they cannot comprehend
the homeless driven by hunger
and terror all across Africa
to camps where millions more
will die from cholera, diarrhea
and numb hopelessness
till the poet runs out of words:
Mother, mother—why
why was I born

> *black? Why*
> *was I born?*

Harambee, my beloved
Africa, *harambee*!
You need not be a continent of refugees.
Five hundred years of slavery
will end when you end them.
They left the chains, but you can make
kitchen utensils of them or
cast them in the sea and take back
your pride. You need not kiss
or grease the hands of any master.
And the fifty flags you inherited
belie your true nature. Banish
the monsters of Mogadishu and
Kigali, Addis Ababa and Bangui,
Moroni, Usumbura and Katanga,
whose fortunes the *mzungu*
propped up without shame.
Slavery is now an affliction
of the mind, and when *uhuru*
echoes through its convoluted
corridors loud enough to command
us all to embrace each other
Africa will be free at last.

> Dance, my beloved
> Africa, dance
> for you are free
> to choose freedom now.
> You cannot live
> on *ugali* or *foufou* alone.
> The joy of life feeds
> on *uhuru*, and *uhuru*
> feeds on knowing
> that you are flying
> at a few hundred km/sec
> through an exploding universe
> that cares for us only
> when we care for each other
> and that like the space
> around us we fly apart

        unless love holds us together.
        Don't let any *toubab* say
        that bringing harmony
        to Africa is like trying
        to play a violin
        by pissing on it.
        Let us join hands
        in a hundred dances
        an ancient courage
        has choreographed
        to confront our enemies
        inside and outside
        the kraal of our skin.

        Sing, my beloved Africa,
        for the riches of the earth
        are still within you—
gold and diamonds, uranium
        phosphates platinum oil
        and iron, waiting
        by a million acres
        of untilled soil
        for you to share
        amongst your people.
        Sing not of pulas
        or dalásis, kwachars
        shillings or zaires—
        sing of the heart's treasures
        and the mind's triumphs,
        sing of Biko and Hani
        and the nameless heroes
        of your many histories,
sing of your rivers and savannahs
        of *babae watolo*, the owl's curse,
        and the blessing of sacred trees
        and mountains, for Africa calls:
        uhuru uhuru uhuru!

The sun has reached its zenith now and the trees
are standing in a pool of their own shade.
The light is so green against a golden sky
I might be living in a hot summer's dream
where lovers float silent as photosynthesis

on the green leaves of their affections,
embracing the knowledge that they go to seed
a new generation, mixing chromosomes with passion
on the off-chance they might surprise the future
and go beyond the stars. Haunted by hummingbirds
viper's bugloss bristles its deep blue forget-me-not
by the pond while in the garden blister beetles
bleed to ward off predators. Like the tawny lily
that blooms for one day only though its green sword
is drawn for the whole season, you and I are
day flowers lost in the wasteland of eternity
with only a song to ward off the night.

6. Across the Sun's Warp

> *When I regard all the world*
> *As my brother*
> *Why is it that its tranquillity*
> *Should be so thoughtlessly disturbed?*
> *Sublime is the moment*
> *When the world is at peace.*
>   *Emperor Hirohito*

Dawn has emerged from a thunderstorm
to the tune of birds rejoicing in the wind
and the tonic rain. Leaf by leaf the light
lowers itself from treetops slides down
the rain's steaming pathways and ignites
green flames we call forests and meadows.
From the thin watercolour hues of dawn
a single hour transmutes the sky into liquid
gold and azure so luminous it seeps into
the crampest of rock crevices, spills into
rodents' burrows in the fields and in cities
splashes around blinds still drawn, flows
soundless under closed doors and bursts
through myriads of windows boisterous
to flood the dark sequestered spaces
we call home—
    but with light comes heat
and heat draws veils of vapour from lakes
and rivers, obscures what's here and now
weighs the mind down with flickering
images of a horror movie: Hiroshima,
mon amour, where seven rivers float
this same morning radiantly down
to Sento Bay into aquamarine lucency.

    August is the month Confucius
    was born who knew to love truth
     is better than to know it as
     the Mayflower set sail from
     Southampton with the truth
   of winds and seas to carry the seeds
   of a new nation and a millennial creed
across the ocean: one-hundred-and-two

           pilgrims who never knew they would
         launch that same month centuries apart
       the Klondike Gold Rush, and Voyager 2
          beyond Jupiter and Saturn,
           and from Tinian Island
         the *Enola Gay* to Hiroshima.
         Thus do fancy and folly
          sit in each other's lap
          and conceive absurdities
             while the sun soars through the lion's constellation
              shaking its golden mane as it travels at 240 km/sec
       230 million years to round the galaxy once, radiating
                2×10^{36} ergs/min into a vast silence to light up
             the solitary planets, give warmth here to grasslands
                   and oceans, wings to birds and insects,
              energy to lovers to pump new life into clouds
                and stones that will in time reclaim them.

          On time's loom nature
      threads stones across the sun's warp
           to weave a garden
        as clouds shuttle the seasons
     and stretch life from birth to death.

Day by day the tilted axis of the world
is spinning night now north of the equator
toward the equinox that must return to darkness
the dominion it maintains throughout the universe.
The sun's shadow unveils the cosmic landscape
for all its sparkling emptiness, its black hostility
to us, to life, even as summer nights take
the luminous pulse of fireflies signalling their passion
to their mates and the low rumble of thunder
promises rain. Sultry midsummer storms drum dawn
into consciousness, the light leaden, the rain black
pearls cascading down the roof, washing memories
heavy with the crude of nightmares to the shores
of awareness, polluting what's familiar, menacing
what's lovable in our green ignorance
till the morning begins to devour the shadows.

It's 8 o'clock. August 6.
This day half a century or so ago
and half a spin of the globe away
the U.S.A. made history a tale
of horror only the most reasonable
of monsters could've invented:
*The Force from which the Sun Draws its Power
Unleashed*
against children on their way
to school or in the classroom
their eyes full of sunshine
curiosity mischief against
student work brigades
of boys and girls assembling
in the city's streets and squares
against doctors teachers nurses—
civilians young and old, sleeping
waking unsuspecting unarmed…
*The Greatest Achievement of Science
Unleashed!*

    Rutherford unravelled the radioactive disintegration
of uranium into beta and gamma rays
at the turn of this blood soaked century
and left us nowhere to hide from a radiance
turned into radiation. He bombarded nitrogen
with energetic radium forcing a proton
from the nucleus to make the alchemists' dream
come true: the transmutation of elements.
Boron into nitrogen into oxygen,
aluminum into phosphorus into silicon—
the atom was split! But the philosopher's stone
Noah hung in the ark to give light
to every creature was found to be
more lethal than a samurai sword.

It must have begun in time immemorial.
Two gods on the floating bridge of heaven
dipped their star-studded spears in the ocean
and created the land of the rising sun. Something
stirred between the clouds and the stones.
Water engendered a genesis both random
and prefigured, a garden rose from the sea

whose freedom inspired cells to arrange
and rearrange themselves in a pattern of mind.
Laboriously, by trial and error, indifferent
to its victims, life wrote its codes of survival
into law as continents moved and seasons
shifted. Against all the odds of climate and
cataclysm the children of the sun spread
till *homo sapiens* reached all the world's coasts.
When the last ice melted, the rising waters
left 3,300 islands stranded in the Pacific and
its inhabitants free to struggle with their own
demons on the narrow road to insight.

> We have walked
> the eightfold way
> of the subatomic world
> and found every particle
> has its anti-particle, every
> electron its positron
> and when they meet
> in their contrariness
> they annihilate each other
> vanishing in a flash
> of energy 90 trillion times
> their mass, leaving
> gamma rays that destroy
> living cells. Einstein
> showed the way
> but couldn't tell why
> all things being equal
> when the yes met the no
> forces in the primal
> clash a dozen or so
> billion years ago
> why anything at all
> was left over
> to constitute matter:
> any electrons muons taus
> and their neutrinos
> any baryons mesons
> or their quarks
> from which to make
> the stars and stones, rivers

fish, flesh and the mind
that wants to know.
The mystery of matter is
itself a question of survival.

How blue and tranquil the sky.
The fussy drone of a bumblebee
more obtrusive than the hum
of a single B-29 superfortress.
There was a war somewhere
all but forgotten in this radiant
dawn and the sirens had sounded
the all-clear. What more
could the heart desire
from a summer's day?
But the morning came up
with a big surprise—the biggest
and bloodiest deception since Troy
was devastated by a horse.

Hahn and Fermi fired neutrons at 15,000 km/sec
like bullets to penetrate the atom's nucleus.
Like gods they created new elements. Uranium
yielded plutonium fissioned into transuranian
unstable elements as neutrons set free fresh neutrons
that freed more neutrons in a resonance process
that triggered a chain reaction that released enough
energy to meet all our needs and fancies on this planet
unto its fiery death. $E=mc^2$ where c is the speed
with which the sun lights and powers the planets
and the space between them, the stones and the clouds,
our flora and fauna, you and me. But the power
proved too much and the light too little for us.
Sicut eritis dei—motto of the blind leading the blind!

What the eye sees and the hand touches
is a construct of the mind, no more,
no less. The eye can scan a seashore
and watch the water shatter in the surf
but it cannot see the architecture in a single
drop or the scheme of molecules in a wave
tenuous and tenacious as a thought. The hand
against the maple trunk can sense the surging

sap, but it cannot feel the turmoil in the tree's
atomic pith any more than the foot can apprehend
the fiery furor at the earth's core. We walk
between dimensions too vast and too minute
for us to encompass though they encompass us.

                    The frenzy of elementary particles are as invisible
to us as the four forces that contain them,
that forever explode and reassemble stars.
What the laughing philosopher thought to be
eternal and indivisible turned out a mad
composition for dancing figures of energy
that made men of reason into monsters figuring
that a kilo of uranium-235 or plutonium-239
could be rigged inside a container to trigger
an explosion that would erase a city in seconds
and incinerate its population, perhaps even
set off a chain reaction that would turn earth
into a supernova fireball. Prometheus' powers
in the hands of madmen. Oppie and his gang
knew the risks but they could only guess
at the reality, and so they built the bomb,
unleashed a force to produce *The Greatest
Simultaneous Slaughter in the Whole History
of Mankind*, turning Hollywood dreams into
a nightmare from which we have yet to awaken.

                At 8:15:17 a.m. the greatest
achievement of science dropped
from the blue and tranquil sky
and exploded precisely as planned
43 seconds later at Long.132°23'29"E
Lat. 34°23'29"N not quite as precisely
as planned for that happened to be
the location of Shima Hospital
whose staff and patients were
instantaneously vaporized
by the forces from which the sun
draws its power. *I've never
felt happier in my life*, said Harry
formally announcing the event.
Joe was furious for having been
bested, and Winston gloated.

> *Little Boy* had spoken and
> the world ended as it had begun
> with a bang and a flash for
> the thousands who witnessed it,
> leaving thousands more to rot
> under a deadly cloud ending
> their happy days with a whimper.

A thunderstorm may clear the air
but it cannot wipe clean the slate
the poet has covered with question
and exclamation marks measuring
the inwit of our kind. The sun
pulls itself up over the horizon
on a dark fury of clouds and inspires
the morning with voices near and far.
The robin trades dulcet phrases
with the light, the chickadees chatter
with the rain that still drips languidly
from leaf to leaf, the imperious bluejays
call their little world stridently to order
and attention—echoes of the chirping
warbling piping whistling musical riot
that greeted us before we could name it
and has accompanied us ever since.
We've come a long way from Africa
since the forests withdrew from us
and we lumbered into the savannah
where we learnt to walk with the sun
and the rains across every continent
to tame oxen and horses, grasses
and trees, which in turn tamed us,
forced us to serve them and build
huts houses villages towns cities
where the tumult of machines
has long made the birds inaudible.

Two fawns break from underbrush
high as hay around my den
flushed by the pressing green
from a jumble of raspberry bushes
ferns goldenrod boneset elecampane
nettles grasses and countless seedlings

of ash cedar elm hemlock and maple.
Their spotted cinnamon fur is
as startling as the sinewed grace
of their movements—abruptly, at short
intervals, their heads jerk erect and
they stand, one leg arrested in mid-air,
stock-still, in mid-motion, intent
on catching a scent, a sign,
the hazel chatoyancy of their eyes
bulging with the strain to see
the unseen, their ears extended
to scoop from the stream of sound
the tiniest atom of danger.
In the heart of such stillness we know
we share the fragility the mystery
and the mind reaches out gives
itself up to an impossible embrace
beyond the indignities and hostilities
survival forces on us. The frisky fawns
leap back into the green waves
of their element at the slightest
smell sound or sight of me.

></br>What if the deer know
> we are no longer at home
> here where we belong
> among the grasses and trees
> home is always a journey.

Hunter-gatherers roamed the islands
of Japan ten thousand years ago
not only in pursuit of fish and flesh,
root and fruit, but on a quest
that took them from pottery to poetry
when they settled down to grow rice
in the warm moist winds blowing
from the sea. As the planet warmed
their hearts warmed to its beauty
and they saw patterns in the caves
of their skulls, brought them outside
and played with them in the light
till they captured something
of the spirit of the rivers on whose banks

they camped and of the mountains
which were sacred, something they felt
but couldn't say except in the play
of lines and shapes in low relief
the Jōmon people indulged
with baroque intricacy on their pots
and later the Yayori tamed
in simpler designs to adorn
the vessels that held wine and water.
Thus they learnt to speak to their gods.
They etched patterns of beauty
into iron and bronze from which they learnt
to make tools—and weapons
for with settlement came possessions
and with possessions war.

>   bronze bells call for peace
>   but peasants with iron swords
>   face in bronze mirrors
>   samurai planting rice and
>   harvesting only corpses.

August 6, 1945, Colonel Tibbets flew a mission
that bore his mother's name: Enola Gay.
He handpicked the B-29 to drop the A-bomb
assembled in sight of the Sangre de Cristo
mountain range at Los Alamos by a crew
of miracle workers with no more scruples
than the chalk they used to scrawl the math
of their inferno on blackboards, no more compassion
than the medical doctors in Dachau conducting
deep-freeze research on prisoners screaming
behind glass walls, or the professors from Kyoto
National University at Unit 731 in Manchuria
infecting POWs with bubonic plague, syphilis
and hemorrhagic fever and dissecting them
still alive to test bacteriological weapons.
In New Mexico they had different names:
like the chutzpa Teller, pusher and puffer
of the bomb (who estimated the risk of blowing up
the planet three in a million and therefore reasonable),
or the sleazy Szilard, too lazy to flush the toilet
(*That's what maids are for!*) but frantic to see the bomb

dropped and collect $750,000 for inventing it—
that's about $2 per head of child woman and man
killed by the bomb (if you include Nagasaki).
Better dead than red—or was it yellow?
Scientists are no more colour-blind than politicians,
and we all know about slit-eyes. *The Japs*, the President
explained, *are beasts and have to be treated as beasts.*
Would Harry vaporize, incinerate or merely flense
the two fawns who prudently slipped back into the fragile
safety of the forest which shelters my home and my mind?

                    Give me the light
                  of compassion to show
                   the trail between fear
                    and greed. Give us
                     the feel of the wind
                   and the taste of rain
                    for a communion
                    with all that lives.
           The petals of every flower
                extract from the sun
                 a colour to love
            and every bird balances
            the universe on the tip
              of its wings. The blue
                 jays are brighter
                 than our ideas
                 and dawn is true.

Is the model we have made of matter more true?
Six leptons and six quarks subjected
to four forces mediated by eight gluons,
two W particles, the Z^o, and the photon.
But what mediates the attraction between
the Milky Way and the Andromeda Galaxy,
the sun and the earth, between you and me?
Let me hold your hand and look in your eyes:
a photon is as weightless as a kiss but
in the world we inhabit love is stronger
than the force between quarks and gluons.
Particles pop into and out of existence from nothing
in fractions of microseconds and you cannot know
where they are if you measure their speed

> but in each other's arms we are the embrace
> where the universe finds temporary peace.
> The three-coloured quarks have no colour
> and their flavours are without taste. Perhaps
> the strange charms of their up and down bottoms
> and tops are strategies of the cosmos to cuckold
> reason.—Three cheers for Mark in Isolde's quark!

Sunflowers shake their heads
in the hot wind that ruffles
the floral plumes of goldenrod.
Briskly hummingbirds zoom
among diminishing flowers.
Like soft purring helicopters
they hover over petal lips
to refuel sweetness and light
with the swiftest of tongue thrusts.
Underground tumescent roots
suck the soil while blueberries
are ripening in the sun and apples
strain the elegance of branches
against another fall. Every hour
creeps closer to the gathering
dark and we must take sides
with the scattered forces of light
to find a way home to the future.

> The brain questing must
> cross its bridges in darkness
> clouds and trees are black
> at night even in moonlight
> bats listen to what they seek.

It is still August 6, 1945—
a date not carved but blasted
forever into the rock of the ages
by an explosion with the force of more
than 12 kilotons of TNT—the full load
of 3,000 B-29 flying fortresses
packed into a single plane
into a single the first atomic bomb.
At 8:16 hours precisely
Little Boy erased Hiroshima.

It was Hitler who promised:
Wir werden ihre Städte ausradieren,
but a B-29 made good on it.

At the instant the bomb's metal casing
was seared into ionized gas by a flash
as hot as the sun's interior and within
0.015 milliseconds a fireball with temperatures
in excess of 300,000° C was born at burst
point (503 m above Shima Hospital)
expanded raced across the stunned city
devouring buildings and people rose
into the sky in a mushroom cloud
and within 10 seconds disappeared
leaving 13 km² of wasteland where children
women and men witnessed the glory
of light absolute as in the forge of stars
at the point and price of death. The fire
that fell from heaven was the fire of hell.
Thousands passed through it so fast their pain
and perplexity never caught up with them
before they vanished forever in a void,
their last image a blinding white-hot blank—
they were the lucky ones.

Luck is as capricious as the light:
both withhold, bestow or withdraw
their favours by happenstance alone.
Outside my window three comfrey
plants hold their white corymbs
high into the August sun.
A foot further east on my path
they would not have survived
the mower past first greening.
By the edge of the pond a heron
sits rigid long enough for a frog
to jump too soon. You, my lucky
reader, and I, your voice, share
our good fortune to be here
now watching the light luxuriate
in a plethora of leaves outside,
then listening to the music of words
as we pursue signs and pointers

on the page promising to bring us
to our senses or our senses to us:
the smell of mint in the garden,
a melody on a violin, the touch
of your lover's hair, the taste
of salt on a seabreeze, the painter's
brush conjuring energy in colour—
but for a different roll of fate's dice
we would have none of it, or we might
have been the melody, the seabreeze,
the brush, or we might have found
ourselves in the hell of Hiroshima—

                    a city born four centuries ago in the shadow
                    of a castle the *damyo* of the Mori clan built
                    by the mouth of the Ōta river. All our cities
                    were built from fear and greed. Peasants,
                    artisans, soldiers, priests and stewards
                    have always flocked to the walls of forts
                    and castles, their numbers growing in proportion
                    to the appetite for power and possessions
                    of the lords and masters who needed them
                    as much as they needed their protection. Fateful
                    symbiosis where blood must flow for peace to reign.

In the beginning the emperor was born
to the goddess of the sun. That's how
Jimmu entered *kam*—apotheosis of all
things majestic extraordinary mysterious:
rivers and mountains, grasses and trees,
the ocean and the sky, the beasts on land
in the sea and in the air. His appointment
was divine: to guide his people *kami
no michi*—in the ways of the gods
to cleanse themselves of pollution
from death and disease, of the stains
of selfish actions, and to build shrines
festooning *torii* and sacred trees
with ropes of straw flying
their prayers on strips of paper to express
their hopes for a good harvest and
their gratitude when it was brought in.
And the Shinto gods were good to Yamamoto

people who danced for the sun goddess
and decorated their majestic burial mounds
with *haniwa* cylinders of rufous-brown clay.

> On the spirit's path
> all that exists is sacred
> clouds stones and trees talk
> of the golden sun dancing
> singing the whole world night long.

The light is now dancing
between bush and tree
from flower to leaf
and across the pond
like a swarm of brimstone
butterflies. The dizzy
velocities of photons
are invisible, resolved
in the greens and yellows
and the blue of a still-life
of heaven and earth
the morning has stretched
across my window.
A covey of ruffed grouse
crosses my footpath
in slow staccato
motion without disturbing
this calm world.
Only my words
come upon its serenity
like a blustering wind
ruffling tranquil
waters. Naming it
we wrench the unnamable
out of shape out of place
we pass judgment
where all is equal.
To speak is to be
human. We inherited
an unnatural order
that forces us to speak
when we should be silent.

　　　　Our first city was the Tower of Babel
　　　　Noah's descendants built to reach heaven.
　　　　But the ancient gods confounded their ambitions
　　　　and turned their language into babble till they
　　　　no longer understood one another or the world.
　　　　Stone by stone and log by beam we have built
　　　　city after city, tied studs and joists and braces
　　　　into frames, placed brick on brick, dug moats
　　　　and sewers, poured concrete, laid out streets
　　　　and squares—only to sack burn raze bomb
　　　　and level them again because who dwell
　　　　in them no longer hear each other in the din
　　　　babble and hubbub of their own making.
　　　　And still we are building cities though the gods
　　　　have long abandoned us, and the cities grow
　　　　larger and their destruction more spectacular,
　　　　more woeful. Ordinary citizens never found
　　　　the safety they sought in their homes that were
　　　　their castles only for those whose homes were
　　　　castles to begin with and even they had to design
　　　　squeaks into their floorboards to foil assassins.
　　　　How to guide the ordinary in the ways
　　　　of *kami*—the extraordinary that we are?

Prince Shōtoku laboured for a whole generation
to frame a constitution that could house a nation
in the way of Buddha, and the sun and the moon
did not lose their brightness when he died,
nor did heaven and earth crumble to ruin
as his people feared. He left behind the blueprint
for a state of harmony and moved on to the next
stage in the cycle of his dying and being
time and again in this blind world of pain
until he might find through enlightenment escape
to a peace absolute in its moveless nothingness.

　　　　If it can be said
　　　　it cannot be true only
　　　　a koan can hint
　　　　at the truth that nothing is
　　　　everything is in Mu.

                America is energy, not contemplation,
                and Manhattan harbours no humility.
                 It feeds on the illusions Hollywood
                    manufactures that life is a movie
                 to be scripted and directed: *Action!*
                   Cut!—action for the hero
                   to punch his way to happiness.
                 The makers of the bomb aimed
                to punch the enemy into submission
                    even if it meant blowing up
                   a couple of hundred thousand
                   women and children—O*rientals*,
                     said Rabi, chief advisor to
                the Manhattan Project, *are not people
                 one loves…I think with my hands.*
               And with their hands they spread death
               from the skies. Bohr and Fermi opposed
                 the bomb they made, demanded a demo
                in the desert for all the world to witness
                 the horror as a warning to make peace.
                   FDR agreed and died, leaving Harry
              to give the green light to General Groves,
                the obese bully in charge of delivering
                   the goods, and he was gung ho
                to drop the bomb on Kyoto to achieve
                maximum casualties and shock, to say
             nothing of the publicity value of obliterating
                three thousand shrines and temples,
             a center of learning, and a chunk of history.
                   Luck and the weather saved Kyoto
                   and sentenced Hiroshima to death.

I walked the path of philosophy between temples
and along a gentle stream in Kyoto, strolled
under the filigree canopy of its colonnades
of cherry trees, leafless in March. A chill wind
was blowing snowflakes like a blizzard of blossoms
through them. It starts at the Inn of the White Sand—
Hashimoto's house filled with poetry and paintings,
Greek pottery, Persian miniatures, and he made
his garden a composition in rock and plant,
tree, sculpture, and their reflections in the pond
through which ponderous koi glide too ancient

for the gaudy colours lavished on them.
Among stone lanterns, iris, lotus flowers, and
trained pines buddhas meditate in bamboo stands
across the centuries. The mind is wedded here
to nature as a boat sailing is to wind and sea.
Into a rock hauled from Kurama on a cart
drawn by four oxen a Chinese hand has chiseled
the characters that inspired Hashimoto,
the painter, as they sustain all civilization:
The Spirit of Art must be Free!

Across the seeker's path the Shōgun Ashikaga
built his silver mansion to indulge his passion
for the moon, for women and tea ceremonies,
which drained him of his silver—except for the sea
of sand whose furrows were sculptured
in his sumptuous garden to ripple the silver
moonlight and pattern the night around
Kagetsudai—the image of Mt. Fuji.
He left Ginkaku to the monks for a temple
where in black lacquered spaces Kan Non,
the goddess of mercy, now dwells with a thousand
statues of Jizo, the guardian god of children.
If they protected the children of Kyoto it was
at the price of Hiroshima's and Nagasaki's:

> Shiguru's incinerated body was identified
> from the lunch box he was still clutching;
> Moto's charred body tagged
> by one lens and one temple of her glasses
> melted to her cheek bones;
> they recognized Kozo's burnt body only
> from the remnants of his boots;
> only the buckle of the belt on Takashi's
> school uniform survived;
> and Yoshika's body was never found,
> only her burnt water bottle—
> school girls and school boys, all of them, thousands of them
> wasted to a triumph of science and politics.

This is the month Blake died
who beheld the universe in a grain
of sand and innocence in a child's
eye, and Conrad who journeyed
into the dark recesses of the human
heart, and Mann who examined
the pact ambition makes with
Mephistopheles, and Balzac who saw
through the human tragicomedy—
they understood that who seeks
knowledge in pursuit of power
comes upon wisdom like a wasp
flying into a spider net: he destroys
it or he will be destroyed by it.
The soft voice of the visionary
goes unheeded in the din of demagogues.
The path to the lighthouse is perilous:
it leads across cliffs at the mercy
of wind and surf to where the keeper
must hold solitary vigil
and send signals into the night
not knowing who receives them—

>   or else the fate of nations
>   is left to the blind and the deaf,
>   the professional self-servers,
>   whether blatant or sophisticated:
>   the academic and the military,
>   Oppenheimer and Groves,
>   the genius and the general,
>   the urbane and the vulgar,
>   chain smoker and teetotaler—
>   an odd couple joined
>   by pride and hubris
>   in a devious scheme.
>   Ignore the signals the mind
>   sends and we are left
>   to inflict on each other
>   the violence of the universe
>   in the tiny spacetime
>   left us for a greater ecstasy.

　　　　　　　The sun is a nuclear holocaust born from a cloud
　　　　　　of dust that extended beyond the most distant planet
　　　　　　and floated in a void until a shock wave from another
　　　　　　distant star exploding set it in slow motion rotating
　　　　　　　faster and faster collapsing for 10 million years
　　　　　　　　till it ignited at the center and our star lit up
　　　　　　　an infrared cocoon where other vortexes of dust
　　　　　　　were rotating collapsing sweeping up the skies
　　　　　　　　spheres too small to start their own fires
　　　　　　fated by chance to be satellites forever of the giant
　　　　　　sun whose body can accommodate a million earths
　　　　　　and whose energies hold the planets in their orbits
　　　　determine their lives, our lives. The light that now thrusts
　　　　　　　　the magenta of a bull thistle's flower into my eyes
　　　　　　was generated at the sun's core before the last ice age,
　　　　　　　before the Gravettians and the wooly mammoths,
　　　　　　　about the time the last Neanderthal died in France.
　　　　　　Temperatures around 15 million degrees still
　　　　　　　accelerate protons in the sun's core to collide
　　　　　　　100 million times a second with enough force
　　　　　　eventually after rebounding septillion times each
　　　　　　　to override their refusal to fuse and surrender
　　　　　　　　the energy that must travel thirty millennia
　　　　　　　to reach the sun's surface which is no surface
　　　　and has no surface for a body would fall through its fire
　　　　faster than through air if it were not instantly vaporized.

　　　　　　　　Sunlight behind leaves
　　　　　　　luminous green on sky blue
　　　　　　　　wind shifting colours
　　　　　　　gestures on a human scale
　　　　　　　　best measure infinity.

Shōtoku's 17 articles brought the great change
for which Kamatari and Naka-no-Ōe built
a city that was to be the center of an empire
where social harmony was to shine like a sun
upon rulers and ruled alike: Nara,
city of timbered temples like music carved
into wood where I walked the path
of history to the Buddha's sublime smile.
A blind priest struggled from China to deliver
his message to the emperor and Shoma

ordered Tōdajii to be built with two pagodas
300 ft tall and the world's greatest hall
to be raised in wood there to be cast
in bronze serenity and peace large enough
to fill the heart of his people. Though
the magic of its gilt *kutsugata* at the corners
of the roof could not fend off the evils of fire
the Daibutsuden endures, its massive beams
darkened with age and incense. In the gentle
geometry of Nara the ways of the gods
converged with wisdom under the lotus tree
in compassion, and a temple to commemorate
the birth of a nation stands as a halfway house
for the weary on their arduous road to the future.

           Is this the story
      of the President's beasts
       and the unlovables
       of atomic physicists
       and trigger-happy
    generals? Or is theirs
the view through the tight
        ass of pride?
      Were the pilgrims
   who landed at Plymouth
   to build the City of God
        bound to leave
     so many wastelands
    at home and abroad?

      When power is
     wedded to faith
      worlds founder
in thunder and lightning.
    There is something
in the logic of unreason
  that turns the heart
to stone. Even Einstein
  supported the bomb
   and lived to regret it
seeing *the drift towards
unparalleled catastrophe.*
Blindness is a condition

        of those (but not only of those)
        who bow their heads before
        the charlatans of ideology
        instead of birdflight and waterfall:
        they turn into terrorists
        because they feed their spirit
        stridency and starve it
        of the silence of trees
        staunchly climbing mountains.

It took 500 flying fortresses and two night raids
on Tokyo by order of General LeMay
to turn streets into rivers of fire
and people into burning matchsticks.
Some of the crews in the B-29s vomited
from the stench of burning flesh filling
the heavens: more than 100,000 civilians
roasted and a million homes torched.
But General Groves determined to out-do
his rivals, out-destroy out-kill
with the mother of all bombs:
        one plane one bomb one flash—
        neat and simple as a Nazi slogan:
        ein Volk ein Reich ein Führer!
        Only the dying was more complex
        more furtive more lingering.

        This war too was waiting in a world
        of privilege and poverty to get started.
        It needed only the crook of a finger
        in Sarajevo to trigger the looping of pride
        and fear back and forth between Vienna
        and Belgrade, Berlin and London,
        Moscow and Paris, feeding the equations
        of greed and hatred back again and again
        into the diplomatic chaos until the fractals
        of war began to emerge in patterns
        of blood—a beauty too terrible for words.
        This is the month the first World War
        started as the misguided masses of Europe
        answered the call *pro patria deoque*
        and began the long march to fifty million
        soldiers' graves that ended at Versailles

              with the signatures of revenge to a treaty
              that guaranteed and delivered another war.

                    If it is true that he
                  who kills moth or butterfly
                     shall never be loved
                      by man or woman,
                  what is to become of those
                  whose riches and reputations
                    were made by the bomb,
                    by any bomb or bullet—
                  what is to become of them,
                         of us all?

Up in that blue and tranquil sky
serene as Buddha's smile
then as now here and there
the Enola Gay is over its target
on Special Mission No.13
and its crew become characters
in a twentieth century Noh play
performing a ritual murder
too stilted for their true emotions:

            Pilot: *We're about to start*
                   the bomb run.
                   Put on your goggles.

            Bombardier: *I've got it.—*
                        Bomb away!.....
                        See anything yet?

            Tail Gunner: *No, sir…* (forty seconds later)
                         Yes, sir!!!
                         A huge circular cloud
                         as if a ring around some distant
                         planet had detached itself
                         and was coming up
                         toward us!

A thunderous shock wave shakes the plane
and lifts it violently up towards the sun.

Pilot: *Flak!!!*

Tail Gunner: *There's another one coming!*

Another shock wave.
Another surge toward the sun.

Pilot: *OK. That was the reflected
       shock wave. There won't be
       any more. Stay calm.*

Tail Gunner: *A column of smoke is rising fast…
       It has a fiery core…Fires
       are springing up everywhere…
       There are too many to count…
       Here it comes—
       the mushroom shape…*

Pilot: *Target visually bombed
       with good results.*

Weaponeer: *Good? Hell—
       results clear-cut!
       Successful in all respects.
       Visual effects greater than
       Alamogordo!*

Pilot: *The destruction is bigger
       than I had really imagined.*

Co-pilot: *My God, what have we done?*

Hiroshima: city and port
spread between two ranges of hills
like an open fan
across the delta of the river Ōta
transformed into an inferno
at exactly 8:16 a.m.
August 6, 1945:
first the flash the *pika*
then the blue whitehot blaze
       that few survived who saw it
then the blast the shock wave

          that perforated human bodies
          even miles away with splinters
          of glass wood stone metal
          like shrapnel
and then the heat wave
          igniting a firestorm
          that raged across the ruins
          two hours later at 65km/h
          and consumed what was left
          of buildings and survivors
          too slow to escape—
waves, circles more deadly
than Dante's hell, rings of destruction:
in a radius of 1 km from ground zero
90% of all living beings killed instantly,
in a radius of 2km
all buildings destroyed,
in a radius of 3km
heat rays caused primary burns—
a circle 10km across left to chaos
a city wasted a desert of rubble
without light or water or food
a hundred thousand children women men
dead or dying that first day
and perhaps as many to die
in the weeks months years to follow
from a disease born like a bolt from heaven
that catastrophic day—radiation sickness:
in the smouldering of the 125-bed
Communications Hospital 2,500 victims
crammed into corridors stairways toilets
without doors or windows with festering
wounds and raw burns vomiting urinating
defecating blood wherever they lay
on filthy tatamis without help or hope
for less than 10% of doctors and nurses
in the city survived the first impact
and they couldn't diagnose the sickness
they had never known or heard of
and they couldn't treat anyone
for there were no medical supplies:
no bandages, no antiseptics, no painkillers…

> My God, what have we done!
> Surely if I can hear the groans and cries
> across half a century and around half the globe
> someone in the ubiquitous order of angels
> should've listened and heard. Instead
> the blue morning mushroomed into a dark
> and noxious cloud from which black rain fell
> and streaked broken walls and stunted trees,
> black raindrops settling on the dying dead
> and living, staining the pure pink of children's
> raw flesh—heaven's answer to their pleas.

Here the morning is a blue scrim
across the sky hiding the stars
and the vast indifferent void between them
only from the truly blind. The storms
of war and youth have long dispersed
the airy angels of my childhood.
Life flickers fragile between nuclear
holocausts and the cosmic deepfreeze
that turns blood to stone.

> How is it men who have mastered
> the mathematics of Armageddon
> cannot put two and two together
> on a sunny August morning?

> The sun's light deceives
> those who seek solace in space
> night rules absolute
> dawn is but a wake-up call
> to find the light inside you.

Did the Empress Shōtoku see the light
in her love for a Buddhist priest
and did Dōkyō see it in his lust for power
that led them to disgrace and murder foul?
Who can look into the seeds of time
and say which will grow and which die?
The seeds of art and music drifted across
the seas from China and took root:
the dulcet song of the five-stringed lute
inlaid with tortoise shell and agate,

carved and coloured masks to dramatize
the dance, the swift and gentle firmness
of the brush on the scroll conjuring
mountains, flowers and the wisdom of sages:

> In the wind's eddies
> cherry blossoms rock and whirl
> their sweet scent wafted
> high on invisible waves
> to ebb away in the sky.

> The eight-armed Buddha with a lotus flower
> who holds out a rope to climb to enlightenment,
> a black pearl in his forehead—a third eye:
> can it see the future in the seed?
> The Sutra of the Golden Light promises
> peace and prosperity to all nations
> on the path of charity and compassion
> where meanness is erased from the heart.
> Imagine light where there is no darkness
> and listen to the 4,500 poems of the Manyōshū
> sing of sun and moon, rivers, trees, the seasons
> of the heart: sorrow yearning love.

And so tradition weaves the centuries together.
The Emperor Kammu moved his court to Kyoto
and put the Fujiwara clan on the throne
for two centuries. Another city was born
whose winging temple roofs forever lift
the mind beyond the raging stars. Men
rehearsed the rules of government and worship
while women tended to the native tongue
recording the memories on which tradition
feeds: court ladies in love with the cuckoo's
call at dawn and anything that cries at night
(except babies), indulging pen and brush
in diaries and pillow books exulting
in the splendour and privilege of their class
which men defined and defended with sword
and statute for the greater benefit of all
who benefited. And Murasaki telling the tale
of Prince Genji's adventures: a woman creating
a universe of emotions in which a man travels

from knowledge of woman to a quest for truth—
never-ending journey of the wondering mind.

                    A millennium later men who never
                    travelled anywhere but to display
                    the void at their core strut
                    across the world stage playing
                    buffoons and barbarians
                    with such aplomb to make
                    this century a season of blood,
            its equinox a sunny August morning
                    at the hour of the dog
                    when they made of Hiroshima
                    the epitome of their own hell:

After the *pikadon* the procession of corpses
survivors picking their way among ruins
burning houses tangles of torn cables
and wires charred shrunken bodies rubble—
slow march of barely human shapes clothes
blasted or burnt off moving as in a nightmare
numb with shock and pain moaning crying
driven by instinct to escape they know not what
the fire the smoke the dust the horror they can't
comprehend women men children flayed alive
their skin hanging in strips from what is left
of their faces their torsos walking zombies
hair torched frizzled shuffling bewildered
schoolgirls their pigtails burnt to crisp stiff horns
holding their arms away from the raw flesh
bleeding blistering some without faces
ears noses lips melted by the fire you can't
tell the back of the head from the front
if it weren't for the moaning: *mizu…mizu…mizu…*—
But there is no water to put out the fires
inside them or outside on their skins in the streets.

           Bashō's frog leapt into the pond
           with a splash that can be heard still
           and will be heard for as long as
           there are knowing ears—like the *pikadon*
           that changed the world forever and
           the bang at the birth of the universe

>   that fills the void still with a hum.
>   The seeker's mind hears the inaudible.

>   Voices bite into this morning's
>   blue serenity. Sound bytes
>   from hell. Replayed over and over.
>   Mizu…mizu…eraiyo…eraiyo…
>   I cannot bear the pain.
>   The sun has climbed into the treetops
>   yet it is still 8:16 a.m.: the flash
>   the blast the firestorm—then the parade
>   of whimpering skeletons. Time
>   stands still where there is no hope.

It is still August 6, 1945
and we have used the half-century since
to stockpile enough nuclear bombs
to fry every city and every citizen
on this planet to a crisp. The tiny pink
flowers of pokeweed have brought forth
poisonous black berries whose carmine
juice yields a dye to paint blood
all over nature's blue-green canvas.

>   Look at your image
>   in the mirror is clouded
>   beauty you can paint
>   only when you break your brush
>   and draw it with empty hands.

>   Force and matter are both
>   a matter of particles. Yet
>   a jackpine cannot occupy
>   the space of a birch. Trees
>   don't add up, nor do flowers
>   or people, but their force
>   does. Mysteriously
>   their integral spin unites
>   bosons to make forests
>   burn hotter and brighter
>   than a match and the larger
>   earth holds back the sea
>   against the moon's pull.

                                    The half integral spin
                                    of fermions condemns
                                    all that exists in bodies
                                    to compete for a place
                                 in the endless cosmic night.

The gardens of Japan transform force
into elegance embodying the asymmetry
of the universe in designs so intricately simple
stream and flower, rock and tree are joined
in music to inspire Heinan nobles to float
poems on lily-padded ponds as they sip
tea or sake, translating passion into decorum.
If there is a way to throw a spear with hands
empty, the Taira and Minamoto warriors
never learnt the art. In bloody disturbances
they took by sword what the brush had
turned into song. Emperors retired to their palace
gardens and ruled for seven hundred years
by counsel and intrigue while shōguns with iron
hand and implacable minds ran the affairs of state.
Between Kamakura and Tokugawa samurai
enforced peace so that the soft strings
of the kōto could learn to ease sorrow
and heighten joy and the thirty-one syllables
of the tanka could capture the seasons:

                Pink blossoms in spring
            in summer the green rice fields
                autumn's ginkgo gold
            and the snowdrifts of winter
              painted with a brush of fire.

                        By bloodshed Yorimoto created order
                        and settled on the archipelago the virtue
                        of justice. The gods sent a typhoon
                        in August—a *kamikaze* to destroy
                        Kublai Khan's fleet, drown his army,
                        and save the people of the rising sun
                        from Mongol slaughter or slavery.
                        Yoshimitsu built a golden pavilion
                        between heaven and earth—
                        a glittering jewel reflecting shōgun
                        refinement in the koi-furrowed lake.

Thus civilization travelled by boat,
on horse-back, by the wise pen
and the bloody sword. The affairs
of men and women have their seasons
too. Harvests of song and dance
alternate with slaughter in battle,
the meditations of the *shakuhachi* flute
give way to the groans of war's victims
till Nobunaga defeated his *damyo* rivals
and set fire to a mountain to rid himself
of Kyoto's meddlesome monks: he killed
tens of thousands of them, their women
and children, then built a tall castle
of stone and wood with moats
and ramparts to withstand the new
weapon: cannons. A Tokugawa tower rose
to guard the sky and the peace that turned
the nation into a strict and exclusive
but caring family functional for three
centuries. Samurai became civil servants
and moved to Edo, a fishing village growing
into a metropolis where Kabuki actors
to the twang of the three-stringed *samisen*
flute, clappers and drums entertained
riotously with tales of star-crossed lovers
come to grief between passion and propriety—
the age-old rocks of tragedy for every
wandering bark. Bashō extracted serene
melancholy from the passage of all things
through the season's filter of images pressed
into the haiku's tight vat. Poets sang and
painters spread life and times across scrolls
of silk and paper as writers plotted between
romance, satire and melodrama, mask,
pantomime and suspense the never-ending
human comedy of fancies and follies.

> It was the merchants forced the last Shōgun
> to resign and Emperor Meiji to throw open
> the gates to the Western world shut tight
> for centuries. And they came from beyond
> the seas with machines and money to haul
> these islands into another age—the industrial
> the technological, the nuclear age!

        The wind and the leaves
        clouds condensing in the air
        fish parting the waves
        my hand fondling your hair—all
        exchanges of energy.

    Matter and energy are two sides of the same embrace.
        The universe may be a tiny bubble of spacetime
    sprung from the void and blown out of all proportions
    and we are inside it, circumscribed by its infinite finity
        and a mind that can no more comprehend its own
    workings than a grape can come to taste its own wine.
        Let us drink to the forces that have filtered
            through space from chaos a moment
            for us to invest with beauty and truth.

The light which paints the morning
landscape across my window and
the warmth that caresses your face
are the remnants of a nuclear holocaust
tamed on its 8½ minute ride to earth;
they were born in a cauldron that burns
700 million tons of hydrogen a second
to fend off the force of gravity
which will some day crush
and leave the sun a black dwarf.
The universe happens
between vast voids by violence,
created on a scale of numbers
that never add up to anything
comprehensible and leave us nothing
but a speck of time and space
to defy it with a gesture of gentleness—
a moment of music, circles of dance
and embrace, unknown
in the brutal gyrations of stars.
So fragile the window for the mind
to reach and wonder, to open
the door a crack and hold its hand
into the mystery and feel something
passing in the dark.

                Bunraku puppets
              Beethoven's *Grosse Fuge*
             the Sistine Chapel—
       voices to touch and move us
    beyond the known and measured.

Goldfinches flit among the flowers of the yellow
goat's beard whose seed-faces are open now
and follow the sun until noon. Across Ontario
children on their vacations are leaping into lakes
and rivers or fishing from boats with their fathers
trawling casting angling while their mothers tan
by the dock. Breakfast is over and life is good.
Countless snapshots will be taken today,
August 6, to hold fast at least 1/100 second
of a smile, of shared sunshine joy and peace.
Where to put these photos in the albums
of so many summers in so many places?

              A ten-year-old bent over
              the burnt and blistered body
              of his dead little sister
              crying: *Mako! Mako!*
              Please don't die!

                        A woman naked raw
                        pink as fried octopus
                        a charred infant still
                        attached to her nipple
                        scrawling her name on a wall
                        with her own blood because
                        her lips are burnt beyond speech.

A man (perhaps) grotesquely
scorched without nose or ears
drinking black blood-stained
vomit water from a reservoir
filled with people boiled alive.

                        Give me back my mother
                        give me back my father
                        give me back my childhood
                        give me back myself...

The President sent *very warm congratulations*
to the General on the success of the A-bomb:
This is the greatest day in history!
and all the President's men cheered.

                        Twelve-year-old Susumu—No no!
                        Don't look at her blistered face
                        so swollen she is blind and mute.
                        Instead, look at the river—No no no!!
                        Don't look at the river log-jammed
                        with bodies…men children women
                        who leapt into the current to cool
                        their burning skin their bleeding
                        perforated limbs and bled to death
                        or drowned…corpses floating in
                        spilled oil blood filth debris…lovers
                        embracing in death… fathers mothers
                        trying to save daughters sons
                        their parents siblings husbands…—
                        No no no no—don't look!!!
                        Don't listen to the groaning
                        whimpering crying…*mizu mizu…*
                        In the metropolis of water…*eraiyo*
                        eraiyo…—Stop up your ears!
                        You must take leave of your senses
                        or you'll smell the sweet fishy stench
                        of burning human flesh. Sore and dazed
                        survivors are already lighting makeshift
                        pyres built from the wreckage of their
                        homes to burn their dead loved ones.
                        Acrid fumes sting your eyes. Close them!
                        Or you'll see the flying ashes take wing
                        swarms of black flies laying eggs
                        in raw wounds that'll soon squirm
                        with nests of maggots.—No. Don't look!
                        There are no ointments no bandages
                        no doctors…no no no—don't listen!
                        Victors never listen never see never
                        speak except of their victory. Be one
                        of them—the three Chinese monkeys!

Thirteen years and a few hundred thousand
victims later Harry wrote the city fathers
of Hiroshima he would do it all over again.
And all the scientists clapped and cheered
Oppie who gave them the boxer's victory salute.
The General was so proud and pleased he rushed
to drop Fat Man on Nagasaki three days later
for a repeat performance of the *pikadon:*
the flash the blast the firestorm—
lest the Japs spoil his triumph and surrender.
And a Talmudic student from a village
in Lithuania came to America, changed
his name to William (the Bard) Leonardo
(the Genius) Laurence (his street), exchanged
Jahweh for Mammon and Mephistopheles:
I am destiny, he wrote in the cockpit of Bock's Car
over Nagasaki as he looked down on *the thousands
of little children who certainly had nothing
to do with the war.... They were like a fatted calf,
you know, saved for the slaughter. I know
they don't know...that this is their last night
on earth.* And Bill exulted—for a fee
he had become the bomb's official panegyrist,
America's nuclear cheer-leader: *Prometheus
brought a new fire down to earth.*

> *I'd like to fly over there,* wrote the mother
> of a GI killed in action in the Pacific, *and drop
> more bombs myself.* Grief can be deadly.
> And she knew nothing of the legions
> of comfort women raped a thousand times
> a day from Korea to the Philippines by Asia's
> master race. Or of the Bataan death march
> of US and Filipino POWs starved and beaten
> to death by their captors. Or of the victorious
> soldiers who bayonetted pregnant women
> in China before roasting them by the pound
> on a spit for supper. *When you deal with beasts
> you have to treat them as beasts. This is
> the happiest day of my life.*

> Don't listen to their words,
> my weary reader, they know not
> what they say. They cannot mean
> what they say. Words streak across
> the mind's night sky like meteors,
> their core fragments of memories
> burning with shame and desire
> fear and pity, dimly lighting up
> the shadows of shapes and figures
> distorted in time's concave optic
> and through the convex lenses
> of tears. There are tears in all things,
> even in the Buddha's smile
> for only their passing is eternal.

This is the month Genghis Khan died
whose hordes conquered Asia
by murder and rape, exterminating
the kingdoms of Xia Xia, Ogodai, Kublai,
spreading a sea of blood across
the mountains of China and Russia's plains
unmatched in seven centuries until the killing
fields of Flanders, Cambodia and Vietnam,
the holocausts in Germany, Russia, China,
the butcheries in Bosnia, Chile, El Salvador
Indonesia, Guatemala, and Rwanda,
the horrors of Dresden and Hiroshima.

> Who will break the killing cycle?
> Beasts have long ritualized their anger.
> They know the future of the fittest
> is a function of the fellowship of all.
> But we feed on the illusion that each
> human is an island unto himself
> each independent and superior.
> And so our B-29s rain burning oil
> and napalm on cities built of bamboo,
> wood, and rice paper to turn them
> into fields of fire, ashes and tears.
> Where the winds and waves of strife
> disrupt peace and even the gods preach
> revenge, spring and summer fall and
> winter turn into seasons of blood.

Don't look back at the ruins of this city
at the foot of the scorched hills of Ushima
under the mushroom cloud, this Pompeii
man-made that preserved not even the agony
of the bodies, only a few shadows—
a human shape standing on a ladder
radiation-seared into concrete, the outline
of a child surprised in the act of being
alive. Don't look back for a black
and gritty rain is coating what is left
of Hiroshima, its dead and its dying,
with a scourge more malignant and terminal
than the plague—a slow tortuous breakdown
in the blood: first petechiae, purple spots
on the skin, then ulcerating gums, mouths,
bloody vomit and diarrhea, fever, anorexia
and oh—the pain the fatigue the despair!
Later more severe internal hemorrhaging,
purpura, finally epilation, total loss of hair—
a halo of death around the grey heads
of children, women, men. For weeks
they perished, for months, thousands.
Years later the bomb was still picking
its victims, even among the unborn.

Cry not for the dead
but for the living. The man
who played the violin
pleaded for the bomb.
When convictions replace
comprehension the hand
that writes poetry
will pull the trigger.
In the thickets of our heart
flowers as beautiful
as lovers and poisonous
as the Destroying Angel
of our woodlands, grow
to monstrous size and shapes
only to perish with us.
A black void spat us
into this blinding light
to wander in a cloud

   of unknowing the opposites
    that cancel each other
  and us when we no longer
   endure and celebrate them.
    Our days are no more
   dependable than our nights.
  The stars deny our existence
   and afford us neither moral
  high-ground nor reality checks.
   We are what we become
    on our solitary travels
  from one darkness to another
     learning to clap
   with one hand applauding
   what is beyond our reach
    while the other reaches
    far beyond its grasp.

I walked the path of peace in Hiroshima
from the coloured neon ads of its downtown
shopping streets reconstructed in the image
of those who destroyed them, past the hysterical
clinking of *pachinko* parlours where the greed
that fuels war makes the poor poorer
and the rich richer, just like wars. You have to
leave them far behind to reach the park of peace
where the bomb's victims have come to rest
in a mound of ashes under charred disfigured
trees in the shadow of the skeletal dome of
technology. An old man on a cane, his face
scarred by fire, his ears burnt off, shuffled
to the cenotaph, dropped a bunch of flowers,
silently, furtively, as he had done, rain or sun,
wind or snow, every day for half a century
because he cannot, will not, forget,
and he is still dying, his heart still singing:

    Give me back my mother
    give me back my father
    give me back my sons and daughters
    give me back myself.

What are the triumphs of science
if they but unleash suffering?
They can only measure the distance
we have travelled from harmony
to hubris. We are destined to search
for a light to chart a course
through this darkness. A single candle
in the heart is worth a billion supernovae
on the other side of the universe.
We are born to hold a candle to the mind
and name the unnamable. No one
will ever see a quark or a black hole:
their mystery is a matter of mathematics.
But the green leaves that'll soon colour
fall are not a formula, nor is the wind
in your hair. Solitary wanderers
whom the light of love shows the way
home, in our embrace we know
the illusions of touch and taste image
scent and song are our real world.

Some mornings never pass
but the earth moves on
spinning us between cosmic fires
through all the seasons of our days,
the years, the aeons in a calendar
calculated well beyond our ken.
The sun has reached its zenith now,
its glare intense enough to buckle
even crack the striae in stones.
The heat is heavy with the weight
of vaporized clouds. The birds
have fallen silent in the trees
sweating in their own shadows.
The land is wearying of the sun
and longs for a season of respite.
Wintergreen shelters its white
and waxy flowers close to the ground
like urns in the axil of its leaves,
harbouring the aroma of succulent
berries redder and sweeter than blood.
A groundhog is feasting in the garden
in anticipation of a long cold sleep.
All is energy. We have yet to provide
for the mind's never-ending quest.

Adako was two years old
when black rain fell on her
in Hiroshima. Ten years later
she fainted in her schoolyard.
Leukemia. Though she folded
9,964 paper cranes
the bomb's radioactive tentacles
took her, 36 cranes short
of longevity. Will science
achieve that too?

Tell the samurai of the world death
is heavier than a mountain when fools
think duty is a feather in their cap.
Today those who grieve are floating paper
boats with burning candles down the Ōta river
to carry the names of the bomb's victims
down to the forgiving sea. But their blood
won't be washed off this century's history.

Tonight I shall go to the city and
in the setting sun leap into the stream
of faces—faces never black or white
but in myriad shades of dusk and dawn,
olive, rosé, brown, grey and ivory,
bobbing adrift on a tide of the world's
unseen and unwept tears past restaurants
and stores, offices, churches and homes, built
from their passion for peace and happiness.
I shall slip through the curtain of their eyes
to browse in their hearts among all the world's
tales of fear and pity, folly and greed
in search of the force that in the starry night
lights a Buddha's smile and powers the future.

A hawk floats past noon
on the sky's blue waters
in circles drifting slowly
across the golden light.
Its shadow passes over
this fading summer's day
like the hand of a ghost.

***

Postscript

Seasons of Blood is a poem I did not seek out. It came to me over a quarter of a century ago in my study in the woodlands of Glengarry County in Eastern Ontario. I was working on a translation/adaptation of Ibsen's *Hedda Gabler* at the time and resented the intrusion. I surrendered to it because it gave me no peace and I thought it would be a short poem in response to the appalling atrocities in El Salvador committed against its people by a fascist dictator aided and abetted by the U.S.A.

I had no idea that it was the beginning of a work that would not let go of me for the rest of my life. Nor did I have any inkling that it would involve travels around the world—to Central America, Africa, Japan, the Middle East and Europe. Its shape as well as the object of its journey revealed themselves only in the process of writing. The seasons provided a framework that links the poem to a pastoral tradition, but it is epic in scope, and the writing of it presented itself often in musical terms—a polyphonic composition that explores the heights and depths of human joy and suffering as I hear them in the symphonies of Gustav Mahler and Dimitri Shostakovich.

Seasons of Blood has become a cycle of poems in search of who we are. To find our bearings is its concern as the imagination explores the four dimensions of our reality: nature (of which we are a part), politics/history (what we have made of the natural order), science (how we understand nature today), and the human mind (as part of this matrix) searching for comprehension and seeking to manipulate it to our advantage. The poem attempts to locate the place we have reached on our journey through this mysterious universe, perhaps to throw some light on a viable path into the future, at a time when all such paths seem to lead into an increasingly ominous darkness.

I am not sure that this poem has finished with me yet. We have moved to the city of Ottawa now, and new perspectives have opened up urging me to continue the quest but with new strategies and a shift in focus. The winter of our civilization is upon us, and time will tell whether any of us are up to that ultimate challenge.

Henry Beissel, Ottawa, May 17, 2011

Previous Poetry Collections by Henry Beissel

Witness the Heart (1963)

New Wings for Icarus (1966)

The World is a Rainbow (1968)

The Price of Morning (transl. Walter Bauer, 1968)

Face on the Dark (1970)

The Salt I Taste (1973)

A Different Sun (transl. Walter Bauer, 1976)

Cantos North (1980, 1982)

Season of Blood (1984)

Poems New and Selected (1987)

Ammonite (1987)

A Thistle in His Mouth (transl. Peter Huchel, 1987)

Stones to Harvest (1987, 1993)

Dying I was Born (1992)

Letters on Birchbark (transl. Uta Regoli, 2000)

The Dragon & the Pearl (2002)

Across the Sun's Warp (2003)

The Meteorology of Love (2010)

Coming to Terms with a Child (2011)